CELEBRATING HOLY COMMUNION

Another factor which offers to focus interest on the Lord's Supper is the continuing contemporary debate about the nature, health, and renewal of the local church community. What is distinctive about Christian community derives in part from the act of Communion at its heart, the vivid and compelling presence of Christ in the midst of his Church, the quality of sharing implied in the actions and symbols of Communion, and the pattern of community offered to the world which anticipates the perfect sharing in the Kingdom of God ... This may be an appropriate time for the Church of Scotland to open a dialogue with itself, if not with other Churches, as to its understanding of Holy Communion and how, while allowing flexibility, it should best be celebrated.

Panel on Worship Report to General Assembly of 2005

CELEBRATING HOLY COMMUNION

The Working Group on the Place and Practice of Holy Communion

SAINT ANDREW PRESS
Edinburgh

First published in 2010 by
SAINT ANDREW PRESS
121 George Street
Edinburgh EH2 4YN

ISBN 978 0 86153 399 2

British Library Cataloguing in Publication Data
A catalogue record for this book is available from the British Library

Typesetting by Waverley Typesetters
Printed and bound by Bell & Bain Ltd, Glasgow

Contents

Introduction

'Celebrating' and 'Holy Communion' are not always in the same sentence in the minds of the membership of the Church of Scotland. Many people's experience of Communion services are of a prevailing mood of solemnity. The proclamation of Christ's death until he comes – the summarising of teaching on Communion practice in 1 Corinthians 11 – is in awe at the cost of the sacrifice. We are saved as we are judged. But celebration is surely also important. There is joy in believing. Death has been overcome and there is a new creation. The Sacrament of the Lord's Supper draws us, by the grace of our Lord Jesus Christ, into a feasting where our sinful past must be laid aside and the life of the reign of God fully anticipated.

This pamphlet has been written both for ministers and people in the Church of Scotland. It is designed to unpack something of the riches within the Sacrament of the Lord's Supper. It keeps within a relatively brief compass; but in any case we would never aspire to comprehend what is at the heart a mystery, the gift of God beyond our total understanding. For all that Word and Sacrament are deeply interwoven, the Lord's Supper, self-evidently, is about much more than words. Nevertheless, this pamphlet is offered as a tool for the Church's mission in which there is a treasured place for the Sacrament.

Ministers of the Church of Scotland are ordained both to preach and to administer, i.e. preside over, the Sacraments. It clearly matters for them to understand their role. Yet the place of those who have not been so ordained is about being more than passive recipients; the worship of God invites full participation. Deep in our history lie the currents of reform which upheld this principle – not least an insistence that the leading of worship should be in language that people could understand

and that voices should be joined in praise of God, in song and prayer. Alas, it has not always been so clear that the inclusiveness of worship is vital to our faith and practice. Leaders of worship can all too easily take over and dominate the flow of action, and those who are led can slip into increasing degrees of passivity. Even so-called creative worship, new styles, can sometimes be the preserve of the few rather than the many. Perhaps what is offered here can help to energise and deepen consciousness of how the body of Christ, which is the church, is an engagement of all playing their respective parts, to the glory of God.

What follows has at first a limited purpose. It is essentially a commentary on just one characteristic order for the celebration of Holy Communion in the Church of Scotland. But in exploring how the event of the Sacrament may be full and engaging – aiming both to tell how things have been, or are at present, and to open up some thinking on how they might be – it invites critical assessment of all contemporary practice within our Church. There are questions in each section to aid discussion among both ministers and people. The preparation and conduct of worship is critical to the Church's life and witness. And what is sought is more than simply a framework of words informed by sound doctrine; there is in addition the language of symbols, body language, movement language, action language and visual language.[1] Ultimately, however we speak and act, worship is an encounter with the living God actively present in our midst. Where we gather to celebrate the Sacrament of the Lord's Supper, Christ also is made known.

PETER DONALD
Convener of the Working Group

1 See Robert Hovda, *Strong, loving and wise: presiding in the liturgy* (Liturgical Press, 1976).

Common Order

The structure of what follows has been shaped around the 'First Order for the Sacrament of the Lord's Supper or Holy Communion' in the book *Common Order*, first published in 1994 and then subsequently with revisions and most recently in 2005. *Common Order* is a collection of texts authorised to model right order and appropriate content for worship within the Church of Scotland.[2] In the Church of Scotland, the degree of prescription with forms of worship is slight when compared with other traditions. The insistence at the Protestant Reformation of the sixteenth century that the Church should be reformed according to the Word of God as contained in Scripture has opened, to an extent, all sorts of possibilities. That momentous break-up of the Western Church saw the promulgation of many different views and understandings. Scotland gained its own book of 'common order' which was frequently printed up until 1645; this was to settle parameters, though not absolutely to oblige ministers to be bound to particular wordings. In 1645, the Directory of Worship drew back even more from stipulating what had to be done, though it still made certain points insistently.[3] Taking this

2 For the story of *Common Order*, see C. Robertson, '*Common Order*: an introduction' in B. D. Spinks and I. D. Torrance (eds), *To glorify God* (T&T Clark, 1999), pp. 1–11. The essay by Bruno Bürki, 'The celebration of the Eucharist' in the same collection of essays locates the *Common Order* approach against a wider Reformed background. The choice of the First Order here is not because it is seen to be prior in any sense of importance, but as it follows a classical pattern, with variants, which gives therefore an excellent starting-point.

3 'The Directory attempted to comprehend the virtues of form and freedom.' R. C. D. Jasper and G. J. Cuming (eds), *Prayers of the Eucharist, Early and Reformed* (2nd edn, Collins, 1980), p. 187.

alongside the evidence of other texts, whether the Books of Discipline of the Reformation period or the liturgical and popular literature of more recent centuries, and also considering our knowledge of what has happened in local practice over the last 450 years, it is certainly the case that the Church of Scotland has had therefore a long tradition of 'unity in diversity', to borrow a modern phrasing. Now, in this present time, the range of diversity will be expanding rather than contracting, for a whole variety of reasons.

There is beauty in diversity. But there is also a question, both within ecumenical conversations and simply within the Church of Scotland, about what limits there may be to that diversity. In times past, such a question aroused the heights of passion. While we may be glad that dialogue is now conducted in more peaceable fashion, the question is not unimportant, and what follows may be regarded as a modest contribution in its consideration. For while there may be considerable variety in the language, the actions and the settings for worship, the impetus also to uphold a 'common order' has its force. What has been published in the name of the Church sets out to be both usable as it is and a starting place for the development of other forms. For *Common Order*, enabling as it does an interplay between the words and actions of leader and people and the common life which follows on gatherings for worship, attempts to bridge the gap between the contemporary context and traditional material, so as to render the experience of worship genuine and renewing. Therefore, it should matter in the devising of alternative orders of worship to appreciate how *Common Order* works, and the commentary here on the First Order for Holy Communion may be a useful tool in that regard. We would trust that new forms of worship will, in like spirit, seek to be true to the Word of God, pastorally sensitive, inclusive, passionate, contextualised.

It is clear that the First Order, as both example and starting point, has not clamped down on the accepted freedom of ministers, together with their people to shape the offering of worship. Rather, it is built on the recognition that we will all seek a measure of order, however worship is led.[4] One final remark at this stage is to recognise how worship feeds our faith understandings. This much has been understood for a very long time, not least around what Prosper of Aquitaine wrote in the fifth century about the *lex orandi* (the rule of prayer).[5] Thus Holy Communion and its place in the church is a matter not only of worship practice, but also of belief. As we give consideration to diversity in worship approaches, we necessarily also come up against significant doctrinal questions with regard to the Sacraments. It is painfully the case that the Sacrament of unity which is the Lord's Supper focuses still major divisions within the church universal. As we turn our attention here to the Lord's Supper in the Church of Scotland, let us pray that our careful reflection on what we do and believe will foster not only joy and commitment among those who worship within our own tradition, but be a gift to the continuing search for renewal in Christ's church in its many traditions. We belong to a household of faith which is 'one, holy, catholic and apostolic'.

4 'The balance between respect for tradition and creative freedom determines whether or not a liturgy is really "received" by the people of God, in other words, whether it really corresponds to the experience of a Christian community prayer.' Max Thurian, 'The Lima Liturgy' in T. F. Best and D. Heller (eds), *Eucharistic Worship in Ecumenical Contexts* (World Council of Churches [WCC], 1998), p. 14.

5 'Look at the sacred witness of the public priestly prayers which, handed down by the apostles, are celebrated in the same way in all the world and in every catholic church, so that the rule of praying should establish the rule of believing.' Quoted in G. Lathrop, 'Knowing something a little: on the role of the *lex orandi* in the search for Christian unity' in T. F. Best and D. Heller (eds), *So we believe, so we pray* (WCC, 1995), p. 38.

Notes for Reading

In what follows, wordings printed in a smaller font, both italic and non-italicised, are taken directly from *Common Order.*

There is thereafter commentary in three sections.

- Section A sets out simply to describe what the words and the action are designed to accomplish.
- Section B moves on to some analytical reflections following on this.
- Section C is more reflective in nature, drawing conclusions and pointing suggestions. To finish with, a single question is offered to stimulate group discussion – together with a single choice of a hymn or Psalm from the *Church Hymnary Fourth Edition* – all in the hope that this work might help to focus issues worth considering.

Footnotes have been kept to a minimum, and do not set out fully to reference the arguments made in the body of the text.

Thanks are due to all the members of the Working Group on the Place and Practice of Holy Communion which began its meetings in 2005, and the Worship and Doctrine Task Group of the Mission and Discipleship Council which has supported this publication. We are grateful to many besides who have contributed their views and insights along the way.

An Order for Worship

Before any book is opened, the minister and people come together.

A. Common worship needs people to come together (cf. 1 Corinthians 11:18, Hebrews 10:25; Psalm 42:4): so we have always believed, for all that in our own day radio, television and the internet have begun to introduce possibilities aside from physical movement! There are, therefore, at the outset issues of access and welcome; there are considerations of the geography and setting of worship; there are questions about personal preparation before any worship begins.

B. Our appreciation of one another's gifts, and our living out of the commandment of love, is enhanced by our physically coming together. Participation in worship across the airwaves or through cable, or through listening to or watching recorded services, is a different experience, although it can be a lifeline to those unable to join the assembled company of the church. We grow as a Christian community as we know one another by face and name, and as together we sing and pray and serve. Thus it matters that attention is given to the inclusion of all. Issues of physical access must be addressed, as likewise issues of sound and visuals for those with impaired senses. In anticipation of sharing bread and wine, consideration should be given to the addressing of dietary issues such as wheat intolerance, or the need to avoid alcohol. Welcome can be extended both personally and by communicating the order of the day through any suitable means, including in print or on screen.

Seating and the arrangement of space are key issues. In the context of the Lord's Supper, historically there have been traditions of taking up special seating arrangements for the sharing of Communion, and the positioning of the table(s) or the dressing of pews are up for consideration here. Within a church building there may be differing degrees of flexibility in the arrangement of furniture and a variety of patterns of movement during a Communion service, in respect both of the minister and the people. Elders or others who may help in the serving of the Supper may take up special places, in line with established traditions. However, reflection around the use of what might look like a 'top table' could take account of what Jesus taught about taking the most important places at a banquet. Interestingly, the dressing of pews in 'houselling cloths' was envisaged as extending the table around the church, once it was decided for practical reasons to serve people in the pews. And if we believe that it is the Lord Jesus himself who invites us to share in the feast, are there ways in which this can be most fully expressed? Perhaps no-one should assume their presiding roles until the 'invitation' has been made in Christ's name, lest a contrary impression of the minister and those on serving duty sitting early in their places be misinterpreted. A sense of every part of the body being equally participants in the celebration is to be encouraged.

Communion services may be held in church buildings and in many other settings. A guiding principle will be to ensure a common belonging and receiving of the fullness of Christ who gives himself for us. For those who physically struggle to come out from their homes, might energy and effort be invested for the sake of including them? Congregational agendas should be diligent in exploring possibilities for arranging special transport for those who need help; or else for regularly taking the celebration of the Sacrament out to those for whom a journey on their part is very difficult or impractical.

There are also issues to be considered in respect of those who for whatever reason join with the worshipping community, but who are not ready to participate fully in the Sacrament. An ancient pattern was that such people would leave the gathering before the celebration began in the latter part of the Sunday service. In our Church, it is the case that some will voluntarily absent themselves when Communion is celebrated; children not being encouraged to participate may be diverted elsewhere; and there have always been circumstances in which it is inappropriate for individuals to count themselves as fully part of a reconciled and reconciling Christian people. What is best? There is a stronger argument for presence than for absence. True, to be present yet unable to take the bread and drink the cup creates an experience of incompleteness; it underlines that one is an outsider. However, the drive of the Sacrament is to bring about a fullness in which all of creation is included! The faithful long for anyone and everyone during their earthly pilgrimage to seek and to find their confirmed sense of call and direction from the Lord of the Church. The preaching of the Word is most powerfully reinforced by the celebration of the Sacrament of the Lord's Supper: the Church would do well to have its doors open.

What are the bars on full participation? The tradition of the Church is that just as preaching calls for a response of faith and life, so the Sacraments are not one-sided events – the conveying of, as it were, magical tokens. In these rituals our salvation is assured, and we might helpfully use the language of 'sign and seal', in that the sharing of bread and wine both points to and truly conveys the body and blood of Christ, with the many layers of meaning implied in that through the evidence of Scripture. More will be said on that below, but the point here is that participation in the Sacrament therefore should not be undertaken lightly or carelessly. There is more here than ordinary food and drink (which, incidentally, are themselves more spiritually significant than we might usually allow for: see section 21 below). The Church therefore encourages preparation and a measure of understanding on the part of those who come to share in the Lord's Supper, and that the fruits of our sacramental sharing be our ongoing participation in the risen life of Christ.

This said, it is important that we reflect carefully – as the Church of Scotland has done, and continues to do – lest we set up barriers of our own making to the growth of the body of Christ. In recent decades there has been much reassessment, for example, of the possibilities for baptised children and for those with learning difficulties to be fully participant members of the Church. Congregations which have little engaged with such issues, despite the encouragement of

General Assemblies, would be advised to do so. There are different issues again for those who find themselves more comfortable to be 'adherents', especially in the Highlands, or with those who only ever come to public worship for the Communion services. At play may be exaggerated concerns about personal worthiness, or patterns of church membership rather deeply coloured by social convention. There is value and importance in congregations facilitating the exploration of how church and membership are to be understood.[6] And then, finally, there are individuals who in some way have broken with the vision of the healed, reconciled community of faith. It is beyond the scope of this pamphlet to explore why excommunications are very rare nowadays in the Church of Scotland (which was not the case in the past), but it can be recognised that there are situations of 'scandal' which would argue for people holding back from full participation in the Sacrament lest there be rank hypocrisy.[7]

C. It is accepted that the minister of Word and Sacrament has a leading role in the coming together of the people of God. But ordination does not convey special powers or recognise superior gifts; rather, it acknowledges gifts and calling accountable both within the local situation and the church catholic (universal). Thus, the minister leads the prayers of the people, glorifying the risen Christ who is met in the sharing of bread and wine, but in no sense is the minister the only person who counts; the Sacrament cannot be celebrated where there are not two or three gathered in Christ's name. And if the minister has a particular responsibility for the shaping of worship, it cannot be argued that this is a matter of personal discretion simply. The celebration of the Sacrament

6 Just as the church is *semper reformanda* (always needing to be reformed), so we are always needing to be converted, i.e. turned anew to Christ. Note, for the avoidance of doubt, that the Church of Scotland does not uphold denominational barriers in respect of participation in the Lord's Supper – see n. 27 below.

7 Note how the historic practice of excommunication was designed towards bringing the offender back into the body of the church – cf. Margo Todd, *The culture of Protestantism in early modern Scotland* (Yale UP, 2002), ch. 3.

which he or she leads is a participation in an authorised service, that is, according to the understanding of the Church of Scotland. In the background are both our own distinctive historical standards and what might be discerned (though therein lies a challenge!) ecumenically to be the tradition of the undivided church. Tradition is a living reality, continually up for reinterpretation, but we reach for communion not only with Christ but with all the faithful, in every time and place. We wrongly close down horizons of hope when we draw into our own corners to fashion worship simply as it suits us.[8]

In conclusion here, then, the setting of the Sacrament of the Lord's Supper is in faithfulness to Christ and in a belonging alongside all who have called upon his name. As we come together for worship, there is therefore utterly a place for awe and reverence as well as for the friendly greeting and support of one another. There are strong arguments for disciplines of preparation, whether through public worship (as happens still especially in the Highlands) and/or in quiet space. And it is worth noting that in addition to prayer, the time for the healing of broken relationships, the restitution of goods and so on are prior to participation in the Sacrament. The Lord's Supper is a sign and seal of that new road of faith, hope and love on which we are to be determined to travel. And it then becomes a source of extraordinary strengthening!

'Will you come and follow me if I but call your name? ...' (*CH4*, no. 533)

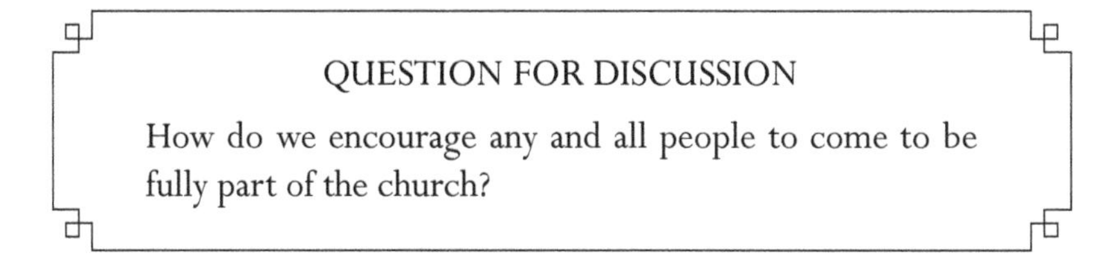

QUESTION FOR DISCUSSION

How do we encourage any and all people to come to be fully part of the church?

8 Note this is still not an argument against flexible forms, only that these forms must be cognisant of core meanings and significances.

1 The Beginning

The Bible is brought into the church. The congregation stands.

A. While an orchestrated procession of the worshipping community as we come together may be rare, in some places there has been a tradition developed of ritually carrying the Scriptures into the church at the outset of worship. The one who is to preach follows in, as a servant of the Word, and the congregation stand in honour of the importance of the Word. Ancient church tradition seems to locate where the thinking originated. The Word of God was to be seen to come into the midst of the assembly. It would be carried, especially for the reading from the Gospels, into a high place (the 'ambo', not unlike a pulpit – historically located somewhere in the midst of the people rather than up at the front), so that there would be a visual showing of the power of the Word which came from above.[9] In Reformed thinking, it was consistent to maintain that the Word should be both read and preached from the same place, whether raised up or not. In that the Church of Scotland has guarded very carefully the need for preachers to be qualified, or under adequate supervision, it has maintained a reverence for that reading and preaching of the Word which was so key an affirmation of the early Reformers.

B. However, it is not maintained that beginning the worship service with the carrying of the Bible is, or must be, done in every place. It would lose

9 Behind church tradition was Jewish practice around the 'bimah'. Over the centuries, the location of the 'ambo', like the location of the pulpit, has moved around.

meaning, for example, if it was done but then the Scriptures were not read or preached from the pulpit – for congregations do use lecterns, or readers and preachers simply hold copies of the Bible in their hands; and sometimes the pulpit Bible is something of an unused relic, brought in and taken out, but never actually used! Pulpits both convey height and enable the best sightlines in certain places; where microphones are not available they offer good acoustic properties. However, they can also be felt to be distant geographically and also conducive to a separation not always helpful between minister and people in the service of worship. Perhaps the Scriptures may be read in the midst, but on ground level, and with the congregation standing, or not; there may be a helpful movement towards the Bible being read from a position in among the worshipping congregation. In many places, pew Bibles are available and people of course bring their own copies with them, to consult in the course of the service.

C. The principle at stake is how we as worshippers allow ourselves to come under the authority of Scripture even from the outset. How we use our worship space, and thinking through how ritual actions convey meaning, is significant. The desire is for a worship service to be more than a gathering for meeting up with one another. We are together to be ready for an encounter with God.

'Jesus calls us here to meet him ...' (*CH4*, no. 510)

QUESTION FOR DISCUSSION

What are the various ways in which we acknowledge the authority of Scripture through the worship service?

2 Call to worship

The minister says:

Let us worship God.

A. The call to worship articulates the common purpose. In form it may be brief, like the text here, or more elaborated. Sometimes there may be an introit piece of music, or an introductory word for that particular Sunday and gathering. However, something critical is lost if the intention of worship is not somehow made clear at the outset. The tradition has been for the minister of Word and Sacrament, if present, to make the point: through Word and Sacrament we shall have our encounter with God.

B. Worship is a corporate act, and the encouragement is there from the outset ('us'). The exploration of ways by which participation and involvement may be maximised is very much a feature of contemporary experience, and it may be fitting, therefore, on occasion for others to initiate the act of worship. There is an argument, if going down this route, for sharing this role widely, so that aside from the minister of Word and Sacrament there is a sense of anyone and everyone having a part in driving the focus of the worshipping assembly. Responsive forms of words can also help here.[10] There may be an anticipation of the theme of the service. Words of welcome are not the point here – or

10 The form frequently used in other churches as well as our own begins, 'The Lord be with you', the congregation replying, 'And with your spirit / and also with you'. There may also be an invocation of the Holy Trinity.

at least, it should be noted, they are something very different: before we were, God was.

C. As human beings we have the capacity to praise God. In this task we are joined in the fullness of time with all creation. Our life is a gift and should not be taken for granted. The call to worship is fundamental, crucial, for the life of the church.

The frequent practice of also issuing words of welcome at the outset deserves some reflection. There is certainly an argument for there to be words of welcome, the putting at ease of strangers and visitors to confirm what welcome they may have received at the doors. In a similar vein, again for the sake of putting at ease those to whom church is a strange place, there may be words which seek to explain without jargon the purpose of the gathering. Others, however, take the opinion that there should be no sense of anyone being a stranger, and that the impression should be avoided of the church being simply a friendly society run by those who hold office. Perhaps on this matter people might agree to differ, except there is a point that something clearly is miscued where the welcome is offered but no call to worship!

'The Lord of heaven confess …' (*CH4*, Psalm 148, at no. 104)

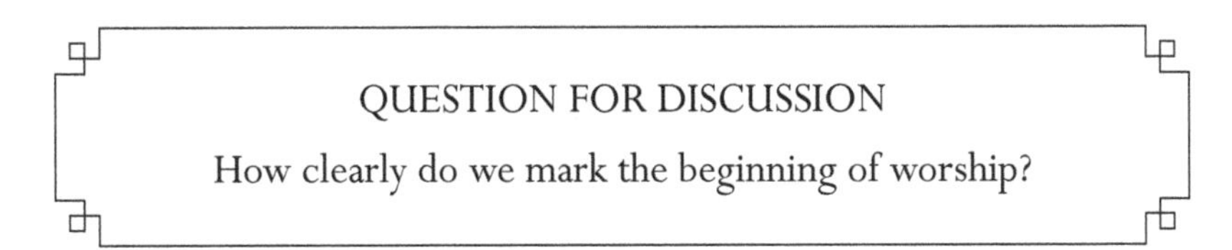

QUESTION FOR DISCUSSION

How clearly do we mark the beginning of worship?

3 Hymn

4 Scripture Sentences (or Seasonal Sentences)

The minister says:

God so loved the world
that he gave his only Son,
that everyone who has faith in him
may not perish but have eternal life.

St John 3:16

It is good to give thanks to the Lord,
for his love endures for ever.

Psalm 106:1

How can I repay the Lord for all his benefits to me?
I will lift up the cup of salvation and call on the Lord by name.
I will pay my vows to the Lord in the presence of all his people.

Psalm 116:12–14

A. Singing encourages the full participation of the gathered people. Here at the opening of the service it is to be assumed that there should be a strong note of praise. The choice of what is sung might take into account what is likely to be familiar as well as questions of connection with the day's theme or the anticipated Sacrament. As far as possible, the corporate singing at this point especially builds belonging. We would wish to avoid creating feelings of alienation and strangeness. We would wish to affirm our service of God.

Following close on the congregational singing, the spoken Word of God is offered to the gathered people. The texts suggested in *Common Order* connect either with the seasonal pattern of readings or with the meaning of the Communion about to be celebrated. Such texts may give a launching point for subsequent prayers or preaching; it is taken that the words here are key to what follows throughout the service. Therefore, there should be careful thought in choosing them.

B. Some may not incline to keep this pairing of praise and Scripture as the preface to public prayer which follows. However, the rooting of the practice is in older (and some contemporary) traditions, where the only praise to be sung in public worship would also itself be Scriptural text, i.e. from the Psalms. Even where songs and hymns are in regular use, some congregations will choose always to begin with a psalm. The thinking, well-rooted in Reformed tradition, is that Scripture has a vital shaping role to all that we do, not least in the worship of God. Our knowledge of God is mediated through the Word which is contained in the Scriptures of the Old and New Testaments. There is good reason to build the familiarity of the people of God with that.

C. Our capacity to pray and praise God's holy name is dependent on the work of the Holy Spirit. Praise is not mere human invention, and we need help with our prayer. Holy Scripture therefore critically shapes and informs our Christian spirituality. Our singing, as our speaking, through worship delights in the interplay of human creativity with divine inspiration. We do well to keep many doors open for the Word to take root in us.

'The Lord's my light and saving health' (Psalm 27 at *CH4*, no. 22)

QUESTION FOR DISCUSSION

How do we bring out connections between the spoken and sung Word?

5 Prayers

The minister says:

Let us pray.

Almighty God,
to whom all hearts are open,
all desires known,
and from whom no secrets are hidden;
cleanse the thoughts of our hearts
by the inspiration of your Holy Spirit,
that we may perfectly love you
and worthily magnify your holy name;
through Christ our Lord.

Most merciful God,
we confess that we have sinned,
in thought, word, and deed,
and in common with others.
We are truly sorry
and turn humbly from our sins.

Lord, have mercy.
Christ, have mercy.
Lord, have mercy.

Almighty God
have mercy upon you,
pardon and deliver you from all your sins,
confirm and strengthen you in all goodness,
and keep you in life eternal,
through Jesus Christ our Lord. ***Amen.***

or

In the name of Jesus Christ,
I declare to you
who have confessed your sin to God
that he of his love
freely forgives you
and absolves you of all your sin.
He offers you now
the grace and strength of his Holy Spirit.
Amen.
Merciful God,
you have prepared for those who love you
such good things as pass human understanding.
Pour into our hearts such love towards you
that we, loving you above all things,
may obtain your promises,
which exceed all that we can desire;
through Jesus Christ our Lord.
Amen.

Collect of the day

6 Gloria in Excelsis

Gloria in Excelsis said or sung

Glory to God in the highest,
and peace to God's people on earth.

Lord God, heavenly king,
almighty God and Father,
we worship you, we give you thanks,
we praise you for your glory.
Lord Jesus Christ, only Son of the Father,

Lord God, Lamb of God,
you take away the sin of the world:
have mercy on us;
you are seated
at the right hand of the Father:
receive our prayer.

For you alone are the Holy One,
you alone are the Lord,
you alone are the Most High,
Jesus Christ,
with the Holy Spirit,
in the glory of God the Father.
Amen.

A. The modern editions of *Common Order* have printed forms of prayers ready for use. There is encouragement here first to pray in a certain pattern. At this point in the service, there is the classic Collect for Purity, a confession of sin and words of absolution and a further Collect, with the suggestion that yet another Collect, appropriate to the season of the Christian year, may follow on the back of that. The people are encouraged to say 'Amen' both after the absolution and after the Collect – though, strangely, not after the opening Collect for Purity. The people are also active speakers or singers of the words 'Christ, have mercy'; and then at the climax, all are invited to join together in saying or singing the 'Gloria in Excelsis'.

The pattern having been set, it can be seen that the dominating note of these forms in sum is a reflection on how the church classically identifies itself, namely as one, holy, catholic and apostolic. Unity is expressed through all the people saying 'Amen'. Holiness is the great concern of the purity prayer. Catholicity, the mark which speaks of the church's wholeness and thus universality over time and space, is signified by the borrowings from hallowed liturgical tradition, the 'Kyrie' ('Lord, have mercy, ***Christ, have mercy***, Lord, have mercy') and the 'Gloria'.[11] And apostolicity, keeping in the line of the apostles, is most obviously signalled through the pattern of confession followed by absolution (cf. Matthew 16:19; John 19:22–3).

B. While some will appreciate the rich heritage signalled within these forms as printed, many are accustomed to a more flexible approach in public prayer, whether in extempore mode, or in borrowing from various sources, so that there is unfamiliarity with the tradition being drawn on here. Furthermore, there is a real problem in that *Common Order* is almost never given into the hands of the people (as opposed to ministers); how then is participation to happen unless by special print runs?[12]

Still, however, there is a case for noting the intentions here in *Common Order*. Where do our prayers begin? If prayers might come between one hymn of praise and another, there is good reason for us to pause on our need of God's grace, and the work of the Holy Spirit in particular, as we join with the communion of saints in worship. If by Christ's extraordinary sacrifice we may approach the mercy-seat, it is by his merits alone. We cannot suppose that we are on a level footing with God. There is an argument then for something other than light familiarity. We open our hearts to God and, though thankful that we may do that without fear, this is, in every sense, awesome. Here is the underpinning of the opening Collect.

Then the confession of sin which follows closely on that recognition of our need of Christ is no less essential. Though there is everything to be said for private preparation to have taken place prior to public worship, this moment for the joint confession of sin is significant, for our walk

11 Both the 'Kyrie' and the 'Gloria' have their origins in the early Church: C. Jones, G. Wainwright, E. Yarnold (eds), *The Study of Liturgy* (SPCK, 1980), pp. 182–3.

12 Those familiar with liturgical forms will recognise that in the Church of England, for example, where the forms of the Collect for Purity and of confession and absolution and the Collect and the Gloria are identical (and perhaps borrowed from?), there is a standard issue of prayer books – as readily available as hymn books. And it is not unknown for such words to appear projected on screens.

with God is communal as well as personal; we may confirm one another in false paths as readily as we uphold one another in goodness. Some churches, including our Reformed forebears, have regarded this shared confession to be essential at the very outset of worship. The saying or singing of 'Lord, have mercy', though potentially formulaic, may also serve the purpose of creating pause and in that pause demanding that we meditate on the ground of our hope, namely that the Lord is merciful and abounding in steadfast love (cf. Psalm 103:8ff.). Such a space for meditation may alternatively be in silence, but we should be clear that our silence is not so much to think on our failures as to think on the goodness of God! The act of confession is about more than trying to work out where we have gone wrong. Because it is confession to God, there is in the very act of confession a moment for guidance and transformation by the One who is ready to forgive. Sin most basically is our drawing away from God. Confession, confessing faith, is our drawing near and discovering that we have been waited for.

God is merciful towards those who turn to Him in penitence and faith, and the delight of the Church is that this should be proclaimed. There are many Biblical texts which can come into use here, as well as words such as those printed in *Common Order*. Church tradition reserves the saying of such words to the people (in the 'you' form) to the one who has been ordained into the ministry of Word and Sacrament, with apostolicity somehow being specially guarded here. However, on the very sound point that apostolicity is as much, if not better, guarded in the keeping of the one apostolic faith by all the people of God, and that the ordained minister is as much in need of saving grace as anyone, the 'us' form may commend itself (whoever utters the words!).[13] Aside from such niceties, it is however very strange if sin is confessed publicly and no words of the comfort of forgiveness expressed. We should not only be privately hopeful that the prayer is answered in God's mercy, but should make that publicly known.

13 *Common Order* does not as such acknowledge this possibility, which is regrettable.

The extension of prayer beyond this corporate time of confession and thankfulness for the mercies of God allows something more of a framing for the service to follow. Hence the borrowing from Collects, short prayers in a certain form but, above all, linking with the liturgical themes of the day. Just as prayers may be said before a service begins with the choir, or with those in leading roles, so the whole community might be blessed through such a prayer as will focus the direction of their having come together. And if this part of prayer leans by what is said in the direction of shaping the worshipping community and preparing it to receive from God, then the notion of ending whatever is prayed with another song of praise takes us back simply and without clutter to the revelation of Christ. 'Glory to God in the highest' is wonderful as a hymn of praise not just because it is ancient; it is full of Scriptural reference. Even if not used on every occasion, it deserves to be a staple for meditation.

C. In the public context, prayers are at the heart of the worshipping experience, for this is not simply a community gathering to bless one another; we are together to bless the name of the Lord. It may be that in wordiness we lay great emphasis on what we have to say to God – and there are things we *have* to say, our confession of sin being well in among that – but we cannot lay aside the understanding that prayer is a two-way exchange. Prayers are not formalities. We are taught to pray because we must: we must relate to God and allow God to relate to us. For the mystery of how God's Word comes to us in prayer, this is the province of the Holy Spirit. On our side, it asks of us to know that prayer is not ended when we have chosen our words (be they ancient or of our own devising) or for that matter regulated music and silences. Prayer is not our work alone.

That said, the prayers of the church must also be more than a monologue on the part of the one who utters them. Public prayers do (or should do) rather more than indulge the spirituality of the one who delivers them. Hence the attraction to traditional forms – but also rightly an interest in enabling everyone to join in. This may be done by sharing texts and having people reading, in unison, part or all of the prayer; but, at the very least, people might confirm their participation by saying 'Amen'. To say 'Amen', the tradition even of Jewish prayer, only became controversial in the Scottish church in the seventeenth century – it was not so in the first phase of the Reformation – and there is much to commend a practice which belies any impression of passivity on those who are not prominent in the assembly. Prayer is not performance; it is actively to connect us with God.

A final word might be offered here about the posture of prayer, though *Common Order* keeps silent about it. Most commonly, heads will be bowed. Perhaps the one who leads may wish to be as physically near the congregation as possible. Ancient tradition would have us pray standing, in reverence and awe, and prayers being sung on the argument that common speech is insufficient; other postures, equally with Biblical foundation, would be kneeling, or with outstretched arms. The question really is that if there is not even an 'Amen' being uttered and people sit in pews or in comfortable, movable seats, are we doing as well as we can to promote prayer as an engagement of body, soul, mind and strength in the love of God?

'Gloria' / 'Gloria', 'Glory to God' (*CH4*, nos 760, 761, 762)

QUESTION FOR DISCUSSION

How can ancient forms of praise help the contemporary church?

7 Old Testament

8 Psalm (*sung or read*)

9 Epistle

10 Gospel (*the congregation may stand*)

11 Alleluia or Hymn

12 Sermon

Before the Sermon this or other prayer is offered.

The minister says:

Let us pray.

God of life and truth,
you have taught us
that we cannot live on bread alone,
but on every word
that comes from the mouth of the Lord.
Feed us with the word of life,
and by your Spirit
lead us into truth;
through Jesus Christ our Lord.
Amen.

This or other Ascription follows the Sermon.

Glory to the Father, and to the Son,
and to the Holy Spirit:
as it was in the beginning, is now,
and will be for ever.
Amen.

A. The reading of Scripture and preaching upon it is ordered as a single piece, with provision for more than one Scriptural passage. In the Revised Common Lectionary, four are possible. One is the Psalm set for that Sunday. The other Old Testament passage has been chosen for its connections either with the Gospel or the other New Testament reading. The reading of the Epistles proceeds continuously, so the set passage may, or may not, connect with the other readings. The intention is that over a three-year period, a substantial part of the canon of Scripture will have been read. As well as offering the suggestion that the Church of Scotland may adopt this 'common' pattern of readings – observed for example in the Church of England and the Roman Catholic Church – *Common Order* further offers some suggestions for performance. It is implied that the reading or singing of the Psalm is an act in which all may actively participate. There is the suggestion that the reading of the Gospel passage may be held in greatest honour, with the people standing as a mark of that, and with a sung Alleluia, or hymn, closely following. There is the expectation that there may be explicit prayer both before and after the sermon, the latter being an ascription of glory to God the Trinity, the former being a prayer for illumination.[14]

B. The use of Scripture in public worship has had a long and varied history. Always there to provide language for praise and prayer, the interplay theologically between the written word of the books of the Bible and Jesus Christ the Word made flesh explains the intensity of the ritual around its reading. It might be thought important to sound the Word from on high, so as to underline its divine origins; the pulpit was a reading desk before it was a preaching platform (cf. above, at the entrance of the Bible). Or, it might be considered important to carry the word physically into the midst of the people, so as to be

14 In the Church's historic standard, the *Westminster Directory of Worship*, the suggested prayers were far more extensive than this, albeit located as they are here. The *Directory* is also fulsome on how the Word should be read and how preached.

clear that Christ came among us; the pattern of standing makes most sense around a movement of the reader plus Bible into the middle of the assembly. There might be incense for Word and people, to measure the holiness of the moment, or candles carried to speak of the light of Christ, but then again the Reformed tradition has feared that excessive ritualising tips into 'superstition'. Another alternative therefore has been to 'translate' in purely a linguistic sense, and there has come to be a multiplicity (in the English language) of Bible translations and the widespread distribution of Bibles literally into everyone's hands. And then the reading of Scripture, said and not sung, may happen from a lectern, a piece of church furniture which had its origins as a music stand from which the whole choir could read from; nowadays, the congregation may follow the text, and read around it, from the comfort of their own seats. Much may be gained in terms of the word being literally close at hand (cf. Deuteronomy 30!) – though, if the danger in former generations was, having ears, not to hear, now the possibility is there of endless dissection of the text *qua* text, or of just closing the book altogether!

If there is something almost sacramental in the opening up of Scripture, the one who reads may help to convey this. The sense that only the sermon needs prayer before and after, as opposed to the readings, is strange. There should be some signal to the hearers that the reading itself is a Christ-event, for it is not the same as reading out of any other book.[15] At the same time, there is something very right about all sorts of church members taking their turn to read the Scriptures, insofar as they have the gift of being able to do this within the gathered assembly. And an Alleluia, or hymns, being sung as links with the readings gives reinforcement to the understanding that all are gathered around this Word which comes 'living and active'. Then, when the sermon is preached, it is good for this to come in the closest

15 At its simplest, it could be 'Let us turn to / hear the Word of God' at the outset, and 'Amen' at the end; but there are many possibilities.

proximity to the readings, lest it be understood to be a different quality of event.[16] It is neither more important than the readings, nor less so. It is another dimension of how Christ teaches and heals and challenges and renews. The one called to preach must be attentive and humble both in preparation and delivery, if the glory indeed is to be given to God.

C. Technology, style and the use of space clearly affect the messages being conveyed. Some will argue for the most effective means of modern communication to be utilised, to help the Word in us bear fruit, but others for the same reason may hold back on some technological innovations. Some will argue for robing and formality and others for casual dress and being conversational, each acting by the light of their perceptions of the church's role in their particular locality. There will be debates about decoration versus plainness, great open spaces versus close and comfortable seating arrangements. In all of this, it matters to be ready for Christ's Word as an event which far outruns anything of our own control, or devising. We are creatures of the Word. In all our creativity, we cannot forget that.

There is the closest of ties between Word and Sacrament. While there may be debates over patterns of readings and styles of preaching – not to mention over what precisely is vital in terms of wording when the Sacraments are celebrated – we should be in no doubt that the grace of God is the same whether unfolded through Word, or sacred sign. It is most helpful therefore that the lines of connection should be drawn even at this stage of the liturgy. How does what we read of, think of, speak of as we turn to the Word of God contained in the Bible connect with the anticipation of Christ's presence in the Lord's Supper? There will be Bible references in plenty as we move to the Sacrament, but there is a sense in which the Word to be preached cannot stand alone. The liturgical pairing of Word and Sacrament expresses profoundly

16 For proximity, the thought might be both of space and time, i.e. where the readings are read, there should the sermon be preached; when the readings are read, then should the sermon be preached.

something of how when Jesus spoke, he also performed signs and wonders; how we are to be not only hearers of the Word, but doers also. Just as the service of God is not ended when the preaching finishes (for the new week is just beginning), the Sacrament will reinforce that point by attuning all our senses to it.

'*Thanks to God whose word was spoken …*' (*CH4*, no. 605)

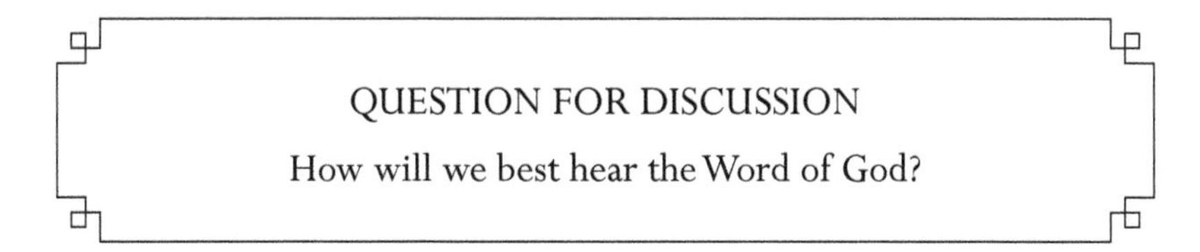

QUESTION FOR DISCUSSION

How will we best hear the Word of God?

13 Nicene Creed

We believe in one God,
the Father, the Almighty,
maker of heaven and earth,
of all that is, seen and unseen.

We believe in one Lord, Jesus Christ,
the only Son of God,
eternally begotten of the Father,
God from God, Light from Light,
true God from true God,
begotten, not made,
of one Being with the Father;
through him all things were made.
For us and for our salvation
he came down from heaven,
was incarnate of the Holy Spirit
and the Virgin Mary
and became truly human.
For our sake he was crucified
under Pontius Pilate;
he suffered death and was buried.
On the third day he rose again
in accordance with the Scriptures;
he ascended into heaven
and is seated at the right hand of the Father.
He will come again in glory
to judge the living and the dead,
and his kingdom will have no end.

We believe in the Holy Spirit,
the Lord, the giver of life,
who proceeds from the Father [and the Son],
who with the Father and the Son
is worshipped and glorified,
who has spoken through the prophets.
We believe in one holy catholic
and apostolic Church.
We acknowledge one baptism
for the forgiveness of sins.
We look for the resurrection of the dead,
and the life of the world to come.
Amen.

14 Hymn

A. *Common Order* here provides for the saying of the so-called 'Nicene Creed' (agreed in fact at the Council of Constantinople in AD 381), and moreover prints a bracketed addition of the ecumenically troublesome 'filioque' clause whereby we say that the Holy Spirit 'proceeds from the Father *and the Son*'. The Creed functions thus to mark the end of the liturgy of the Word, though there is also provision for the singing of a hymn. As the proclamation of the Word has referred the worshipping community to the life of Christ coming into the world, the Creed is a defiant statement for taking into the world the church's orthodoxy, i.e. right belief. God the Father is the Creator; Jesus Christ is the Lord, the Son of God; the Holy Spirit is the Lord, the giver of life. The church is not an article of belief in the same sense (and the translation of the Creed may mislead here); rather, it is marked by its unity, holiness, catholicity and apostolicity, and in our experience we live between baptism and our hope of the resurrection. In the original form the Creed was always expressed personally, as 'I believe', but we should note how this did not imply faith rested on something as fragile as a personal opinion, rather my ownership of the faith allied itself with the faith of the church (agreed in ecumenical council as a symbol of what was accepted by the believers at large). To confess Jesus Christ as Lord was the starting point (cf. Romans 10:9); the faith of the church was the enlargement on that necessitated by everything from heresy to unbelief. The modern preference for 'we believe' is presumably intended as a guard against the individualist fallacy, namely that a person need believe simply in what seems right to that person, which clearly opens major possibilities of challenge to confessing Jesus Christ as Lord. 'We believe' should not be read, said, or sung to imply that my commitment to 'what must be believed' is an option.[17]

B. The content of the Creed repays study, not least because its categories are to an extent alien to contemporary modes of thought, but more that

17 In the Church of Scotland, debates over the *Westminster Confession of Faith* in the nineteenth century settled on a phrase 'the substance of the faith' as a reference point for 'what must be believed'. In the continuing debates over what exactly this refers to, part of the difficulty is a justified resistance on the part of the church to solve it by some formula of words – for we do not worship words, we serve the Word made flesh, Jesus Christ our Lord! Classically, the Nicene Creed has been referred to as a 'symbol' of the faith, thus very definitely pointing to what faith is at its heart, and therefore the onus is on the challengers of the validity of that symbol to come up with a better alternative. In the Reformation, Confessions of Faith were the defiant articulations of the day, aimed at heresy and unbelief, but they were not intended to supplant the Nicene Creed. Likewise, the first Article Declaratory of the 1921 constitution of the Church of Scotland, doxological in character, bears strongly the imprint of Nicene theology. There is truth in the observation that the categories of Nicene faith belong to the early centuries of church history, but there is also truth in the recognition that nearly all the possible variations on Christian faith and challenges to it were raised in the very same period, and thus it has lasting validity!

as its authority derives from its ecumenical significance, it provides a continuing stimulus to dialogue between Christians of all sorts.[18] At the same time, however, it has been well said that it is there to be sung as much as to be analysed – which is to say that it is a gift to the church.[19] Yet in practice, theological formation through singing within the Church of Scotland is weighted more regularly on the hymns and songs chosen for singing than on weekly or even quarterly familiarity with the Creed, which is a point worthy of reflection. (Also, where creedal formulations have had a significant place in the life of the Church – in catechesis and around baptism – the Church of Scotland and the Reformed tradition has most often put an emphasis on the Apostles' Creed.) We may have good reason for finding the Nicene Creed itself a challenge to introduce where it is unfamiliar, but awareness of its authority may well be of use in determining what singing is encouraged by church leaders as worthy of familiarisation. Or perhaps a singable version of the Creed itself is a good way in?

The classic Reformed confessions of faith were not composed for liturgical use, but there have been many alternative creedal forms composed, into recent times. These may well be used in place of the historic symbol of the Nicene Creed, with the thought being that they can be picked up and referred to without too many layers of interpretation.[20] However, they will also need to be studied for their compatibility with Scripture and the faith to which the Nicene Creed bears witness. In favour of the older text is the value of confessing the faith in categories shared not only across space, i.e. other Christians in today's world, but also across time, i.e. with those who have run the

18 See *Confessing the One Faith* (WCC, 1991) for evidence of a stage of dialogue among theologians of international stature.

19 Cf. J. Zizioulas, at Santiago de Compostela, 1993. T. F. Best and G. Gassmann (eds), *On the Way to Fuller Koinonia* (WCC, 1994), p. 108.

20 *Common Order* published, in its endcovers, at one end the Nicene Creed and at the other end the Statement of Faith approved for use by the General Assembly of 1992.

good race before us. As the Sacrament of the Lord's Supper is set to unite us in a communion of saints anticipating the heavenly banquet, there are arguments for keeping with the ecumenical symbol. If there have been tendencies altogether to avoid the liturgical use of creedal forms, perhaps we might pause to reconsider.[21]

C. The church's historic concerns over orthodoxy fall nowadays alongside concerns for so-called 'orthopraxis' and for 'right feelings' (orthopathy?). There have been suspicions that dogmatic teaching is insensitive to issues on the ground and that such issues as abortion or homosexuality, for example, can scarcely be settled by reference to the Nicene Creed; to be 'dogmatic' rings as a term of criticism. On the matter of feelings, the critique would be that the classic themes of theological reflection encourages an over-emphasis on cerebral issues and is poor if not incompetent with regard to the significant arena of human emotions. And then, on the text of the Creed itself, there is a whole series of contemporary questions – like, how did God make all things? Was there a Virgin birth? How does the Holy Spirit speak now? How exactly is the church one or holy or catholic or apostolic?

Is the saying or singing of the Creed then hopelessly outdated? A response on this might first of all underline the Creed's function within worship. Following as it does on the reading and preaching of the Word, where there is every reason to explore life and work issues, not to mention questions of happiness and the fulfilment of the human person, the Creed, by fixing its attention on the God to be worshipped and glorified, is sound in its intentions. The revelation of God is at the

21 In certain church traditions, the Creed is reckoned to be absolutely necessary within the Eucharistic service. The early generations of Reformers – Luther, Zwingli, Bucer, Calvin, Knox – all, without exception, endorsed the use of creeds. Only from the seventeenth century, perhaps with a fear of 'superstition', and people being brought unknowingly along a path which did not match their sense of personal commitment, did the practice fade away. Nowadays, however, a different danger may be present, namely ignorance in respect of the rooting of Christian faith.

heart of Christianity and what it means to be a human person must always come back to that. If dogmatic considerations have earned a bad name, they need to be rescued, not dispensed with. Furthermore, as already mentioned, while the Creed affirms our belonging to God, it is by definition a counterblast to those who say there is no God. As the worshipping community takes up this song, there is something formational here. It is one of many points at which worship may be seen to be counterintuitive, even subversive, in the sense of undercutting alternative patterns of life and thought. And this is still not to foreclose on legitimate areas of theological debate in dialogue with the Creed's specific affirmations.

'We believe in one God' (*CH4*, no. 649)

QUESTION FOR DISCUSSION

How prepared are we to talk about the substance of the faith?

15 Intimations

16 Prayers

The minister says:

Let us pray.

God of faith and love,
by your grace alone
we are called to be your people.
As members of the Christian family in this place,
we pray for the whole Church of Jesus Christ.
Take from her all that disrupts her unity,
and make her faithful in your service.
May your people so live in Christ
and he in them,
that they may be his body in the world today.

We pray for the world which you love,
and for which Christ gave his life.
Guide the leaders of the nations
and all who strive for peace and justice.
Look in mercy on all who are powerless,
and shelter those who are homeless,
hungry, or oppressed.
Help us to care for our neighbours
and to cherish the life of your creation,
that your will may be done on earth.

We pray for our nation.
Bless the Queen and the Royal Family.
Direct the Government, members of Parliament,

and all who in various ways
serve the community.
Grant that none in our land
may be despised or rejected,
and that your kingdom of love may prevail.
We pray for those in need,
for ill or distressed people,
and for those who draw near to death.
In the name of him who bears our griefs
and carries our sorrows,
bring them your comfort and peace.

We give you thanks
for all who have departed this life in faith.
Keep us with them in communion
with Christ our risen Lord,
and bring us at the last with all your saints
to eat and drink
in the glory of your eternal kingdom;
through Jesus Christ,
to whom with you, Father, and the Holy Spirit,
be praise and honour for ever.
Amen.

A. Are intimations part of the worship service? Here is a suggestion that they may be, presumably on the sound reasoning that the service of God will continue 'in spirit and truth' after the liturgy is over. Being placed before the prayers of intercession, they allow aspects of the life of the local church to be noted prior to the sharing of these weekly prayers. That said, there is then something incongruous in the prayers having a preset form, which may but probably will not succeed in taking within their scope the up-to-date points for prayer!

B. The prayers are petitions for church and for world, and so there is expressed concern for unity and prayer for the vulnerable and for the stewardship of the creation; there are prayers for rulers and for those in distress; there is thanksgiving for the faithful departed. As before, the congregation is invited to join in by saying the 'Amen'.

C. The form of intercessory prayer matters rather less than that prayers should be offered, and there is something appropriate in these following on the ministry of the Word. As the Word evokes faith and stirs to action and is responsive to feelings, and as God's very being draws on our commitment, so the work of the people of God roots itself in prayer. The community may be blessed in hearing different voices to lead these prayers, just as a lively responsiveness to local and wider needs of the day may enhance the time given to them. In some situations, 'intimations' may include opportunity for members present to intimate concerns and news, i.e. say, aside from the scheduling of the next Congregational Board meeting; there is then a valuable sense in which prayer picks up from as it were the newspaper in one hand and the Bible in the other.[22] The school of thought that prefers a fixed form, as is offered in *Common Order*, honours the desirability of a pattern where certain people and concerns will always be prayed for, and never omitted. The heart for Christian unity allies itself not least with the so-called high priestly prayer of Jesus in John 17; the prayers for the world take up classic themes frequently alluded to in the Prophets; the prayer for rulers is faithful to the spirit expressed more than once in the Epistles; prayers for those who suffer and mourn return to areas of active concern in Jesus' ministry; the closing petition prays through our belief in communion across not only space but time.

This all said, there might nevertheless be a question as to whether the placing of prayers of intercession at this point in the Communion service, not to mention intimations, is beyond discussion. Thanksgiving

22 This may suggest that the intimations to be underlined and prayed through are those which truly take the worshipping and witnessing community out into the life of the world.

and intercession are a rich pairing,[23] and in the Lord's Supper, the major thanksgiving prayer has not yet been offered. While intercessions very properly are lifted up in response to the preaching of the Word, on this occasion the Word will be held up and strengthened by the sharing around the table yet to come. Our prayers might wait for that time of closeness to our Lord.

There may be another reason for proceeding immediately into the celebration of the Sacrament once the ministry of the Word has been rounded off. The flow of worship has an impact on those who participate. If there are stops and starts, or perceived discontinuities, focus can be lost and distractions given a way in. The invitation to the Lord's Supper may readily pick up from the sharing of the Word. There may be days when it is less connectable with the prayers of intercession.

'For the world and all its people, we address our prayers to God'
(*CH4*, no. 262)

QUESTION FOR DISCUSSION

How and when will we frame our prayers for church and world?

23 Cf. C. Giraudo, 'The Eucharist as *Diakonia*' in K. Pecklers (ed.), *Liturgy in a postmodern world* (Continuum, 2003), p. 105.

17 Invitation

The minister says:

This is the Lord's table.
The Lord Jesus invites us
to share this joyful feast.
From east and west, from north and south,
people will come and take their places
at the banquet in the kingdom of God.

St Luke 13:29

either

Jesus said,
'Come to me, all who are weary
and whose load is heavy;
I will give you rest.
Take my yoke upon you, and learn from me,
for I am gentle and humble-hearted;
and you will find rest for your souls.'

St Matthew 11:28–9

or

Jesus said,
'I am the bread of life.
Whoever comes to me will never be hungry,
and whoever believes in me will never be thirsty.'

St John 6:35

or

Jesus said,
'Blessed are those who hunger and thirst
to see right prevail;
they shall be satisfied.'

St Matthew 5:6

A. The point at which the service now moves into the celebration of the Lord's Supper is a significant change of gear. The host is named, the invitation is uttered in his name, and Scripture is quoted in plenty. This move, highlighting words of Jesus and omitting entirely what used to be the tradition of an exhortation to take care lest the Sacrament be approached too lightly, gives the strongest possible emphasis to the eschatological vision, whereby the Saviour's will is to invite all to the feast.

B. In ancient church tradition, the catechumens would be asked to leave once the service of the Word was over (usually before the saying of the Creed); in Reformation history, texts were composed which likewise were designed to signal who should participate at the table, and who not. Many independent churches will have a separate Communion service after the morning worship, again for the sake of making distinctions. In Church of Scotland history, words here above all, used to focus on the need for self-examination before participation in the Sacrament, since dishonour to the presence of Christ and the essential calling of the church was utterly to be avoided (cf. 1 Corinthians 11:27–31). Known as 'fencing the table', the practice of elders visiting likely communicants in advance of the celebration of the Sacrament, and the preparatory services on the days before Communion, also tied in here. There developed traditions of Communion tokens, later replaced by Communion cards, awarded to those in good standing and with an active faith, for as communicants moved to sit around the table, these tokens would be surrendered as a secondary check on an individual's response to the Minister's words of invitation. And even then the preparation was not regarded as complete; a particular Communion homily would also traditionally have been given around the table to those seated there, distinct from the earlier preaching of the Word.

The context for the invitation texts nowadays is one in which Communion cards are no longer essential, and even where they are still used, they are regularly given out with very little heed to matters of ecclesiastical 'discipline'.[24] Moreover, the geography of Communion services in churches has generally been altered, with tables rarely large enough for substantial numbers to sit around and Communion very frequently being served to people in their ordinary seats or pews. The permission given under certain constraints for children to participate fully has opened questions not raised in earlier Church of Scotland history, including probing the significance of baptism aside from an individual's public profession of faith as the marker of full participation in Communion.[25] The question which lingers, and which in practice is often referred to, is not so much *whether* the Sacrament as food for the journey therefore is open to anyone and everyone, but *on what terms* that might be understood to be the case. Opinions clearly vary. Some have great hesitations about drawing lines of exclusion, building on the memory of Jesus who so frequently broke boundaries and even at the

24 For 'discipline' here, there is an implication of accountability both to Christ and his Church in regard of personal faithfulness. Historically, there was undoubtedly more discipline on matters of a sexual nature than on other matters, and something of a collapse in this whole area which coincided with expansions of urban populations and the impact of the Enlightenment. Nowadays, spiritual disciplines tend to be thought of more as a matter of personal discipleship than of ecclesiastical enforcement; but there remains a fertile area for reflection here.

25 The issue of children is picked up both in the accompanying CD-ROM and in the Report of the General Assembly of 2009. The connections between baptism and participation in Communion, which has received some attention ecumenically, is still in need of further work within the Church of Scotland. Cf. *Becoming a Christian* (WCC, 1999).

Last Supper included Judas and the others who would so shortly after betray him. Thus, on the presumption that the Lord himself is the host, it is said that the Church should not draw any lines of who is in or out at this or any meal; there should be no vetting of whomsoever the Lord draws into his company. At the same time, and with a much longer historical pedigree, there is concern that the Church, in holding to the tradition which came from the Lord himself (1 Corinthians 11:23), has an obligation to promote holiness where sin is all too likely to get a hold. In Jesus' ministry, there was as much correction and chastening as there were surprising inclusions, and the witness of the New Testament letters, and the history of the church ever since, give compelling evidence of corruptive influences and devilish intrigue being frequent aspects within the community of Christians as well as outside it. Thus, on the presumption that 'the Devil . . . prowls around, seeking someone to devour' (cf. 1 Peter 5:8; Psalm 91), the Church has a duty for the sake of the love of God to warn against this; grace was not, nor is, cheap, and to introduce talk of judgement is still compatible with an ultimate or, better, eschatological faith in inclusion.[26]

C. That the invitation comes from the Lord himself relativises the Church's ownership of what is done[27] and also therefore any absolute claims as to one form or another being the ultimate expression of the Lord's Supper. Our accountability to Christ matters at the very same time as

26 Cf. D. Bonhoeffer, *The Cost of Discipleship* (SCM, 1959); M. Volf, *Exclusion and Embrace* (Abingdon Press, 1996). It still has to be admitted that the Church's historical record of inclusion and valuing any and everyone is far from unimpeachable – as liberation and feminist critiques have been right to observe.

27 Earlier guidelines (e.g. Cox) suggested that 'full' members only were admitted but Weatherhead's simple 'members of other Christian Churches are eligible to take communion in the Church of Scotland' reflects the way in which the door has been opening in terms of church law. The legislation on children's participation accorded authority to the Kirk Session to oversee the admission of children who had been baptised but who had not entered formal membership of the Church. *General Assembly Reports*, 1991.

his welcome and encouragement. It may be very good then to combine urging and honesty, directness and welcome. There may or may not be movement consequent on the invitation, in terms of people coming into a new configuration to be around the table,[28] but there should be no sense that the meal, and our participation in it, is taken for granted.

Whether Scripture alone is used at the invitation, or together with exhortatory words spelling out, in some way, the spirit which those who are about to receive should adopt, a variation of such texts, or at the very least an immediacy in their delivery, is highly desirable, again for the sake of underscoring that the Supper is an event, not an accidental extra for those who find themselves there.[29]

There is a strong case for the one who presides at the meal being the one to articulate the invitation. The celebration of the Sacrament has something of a unity from here on and that can be visibly expressed through a single figure being the one among the many. In many situations the same person will already have preached, and may be also the Moderator of the Kirk Session which is responsible for dealing with local confirmation issues. However, others may wish to delight in the body of Christ being one but with many members, and if everyone is clear on their respective roles, there is something lovely about that being visibly expressed. The Church of Scotland retains the position that the one ordained to a ministry of Word and Sacrament is alone

28 The most common Church of Scotland pattern of there being no movement to approach or come round the Table is not shared by many other churches, and owes much to nineteenth-century innovation introduced as much on pragmatic as on theological considerations. Leigh Eric Schmidt, *Holy Fairs* (Princeton UP, 1989).

29 Aside from the *Common Order* alternatives, texts both Biblical and exhortatory may present themselves, depending on what has preceded in the preaching of the Word. John Knox's Exhortation in the 1564 *Book of Common Order* can be found conveniently on the Church of Scotland website, in the Worship and Doctrine pages: www.churchofscotland.org.uk. William Barclay seems to have composed one of the most popular alternatives: 'Come to this table, not because you must but because you may . . .', *The Lord's Supper* (SCM, 1967). See also Robert Pickles' essay on the CD-ROM.

competent to preside over the meal, but there is perhaps more room than usually recognised for the active participation of others long before the bread and wine are physically distributed.[30] Even if only words of eschatological invitation are used, as suggested in *Common Order*, so as to emphasise as strongly as possible that the one who invites speaks on the Lord's behalf, still we might pause to reflect on what we reserve to the other ordained persons among those present, not to mention others.[31]

A final thought might be on the tone of the invitation. By its very nature, an invitation carries promise of things to come, and in its welcome an excitement and expectancy about what will be the outcome of accepting. Can that be conveyed? The invitation is to a joyful feast. Solemnity and dignity are not enemies of joy but they can become so. There is something to be avoided here. Then again, joy is not frivolity. It is built not on our mood but on the gift of faith in the Lord who saves.

'Let us build a house where love can dwell' (*CH4*, no. 198)

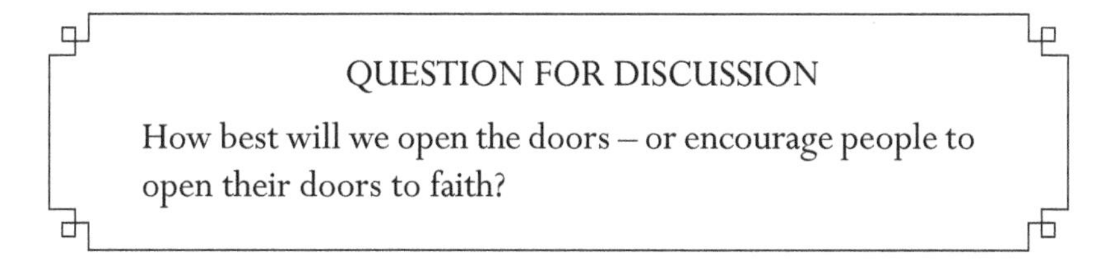

QUESTION FOR DISCUSSION

How best will we open the doors – or encourage people to open their doors to faith?

30 Work continues on questions of ordination and how it confers and authorises. See meanwhile *General Assembly Reports*, 2000 and 2001 (Panel on Doctrine).

31 For example, in the understanding that Christ comes among us as one who serves, there is strong argument for the visible, and perhaps audible, show of participation on the part of the diaconal ministry of ordained deacon or elder. See also below on 'The Distribution of the Elements'.

18 The Offering

19 The Great Entrance

During the singing of a psalm or hymn, the offerings of money, along with the gifts of bread and wine, are brought to the Communion Table.

A. Why the Offering at this point? This is not just finding a place for uplifting and presenting the offering but relates to the sacramental act. In early liturgies, as well as bread and wine other gifts were brought to the table, such as honey and cheese,[32] to be distributed later to the poor. In the West, the focus came to be on the elaborate preparation of the bread and wine. The Reformers were wary of anything which seemed to suggest that what was being offered was in itself a propitiatory sacrifice, so that this episode gave way before a new emphasis, not on the preparation of the bread and wine but of the congregation, so that they could worthily partake. In the second English Prayer Book of 1552, used in Scotland leading up to and a little beyond the Reformation, an offering of money was also substituted, an act which subsequently found its way into other services, expressing the connection between worship and life. In Scotland there was a tradition of making a Communion collection for the poor, and though in 1573, and subsequently, Acts of Assembly stipulated that it be taken at the door of the church rather than at the tables, it would seem that

32 See *Apostolic Tradition* in Cuming and Jasper (eds), *Prayers of the Eucharist*, pp. 21–5. Milk and honey for those newly baptised spoke of entrance into the Promised Land. Benedict XVI in the Encyclical *Sacramentum Caritatis*, para. 47 notes: 'we also bring to the altar all the pain and suffering of the world'.

this regulation was frequently flouted.[33] (See further at section 21 The Unveiling of the Elements.) The perceived danger, currently as well as historically, was that the giving of money might take over from being only part of what is implied in our service to God; it has its place, but it should not be exalted – especially not in relation to the giving of ourselves.

The suggestion in *Common Order* is that the offering should be brought up together with the bread and wine, in that there is a common theme of giving and giftedness (see further at section 21 below). The procession itself, sometimes thought of as quintessentially Scottish, has echoes of ancient tradition. Justin Martyr in the second century describes such a procession; Augustine (354–430) describes the practice of singing to accompany the movement. In the West for a time, the bread and wine were brought forward by members of the congregation, enough for the purpose; in the East, they were prepared in another place and brought, by clergy only, in an action known then as the Great Entrance – at first in a functional and low-key mode but by the sixth century with some ceremony. The Scottish Reformed version was to carry in the plates and cups at the due time so as to place them on the long table(s) at which minister and people would sit. Since more recently tables have in most places been replaced by a single table altar-style in the chancel, the ceremonious dimension has probably been enlarged. The singing of part of Psalm 24 to the tune of St George's, Edinburgh, adds to such an effect.[34]

B. On the matter of processing, whether with money or bread and wine, there is a need for careful thought about what is being signified, not least since local church practices can be experienced as oppressive as well as liberating. Some of the original thinking around raising

33 For ancient precedents, see Justin Martyr in Cuming and Jasper, *Prayers of the Eucharist*, p. 20.

34 Prior to the composing of 'Ye gates' to this setting, the frequent tradition was to sing the 35th Paraphrase prior to the Lord's Supper.

the significance of the Great Entrance was to create echoes of Jesus' entry into Jerusalem, his going to his passion, and the laying of his body in the tomb. Those involved in the representational movements would be suitably attired. With reticence in our Church about this being overdone, one line of thought would suggest that as Word and Sacrament belong intimately together, Bible and Communion vessels should be present for the whole service and, for practical reasons, thus even if the Bible will be carried in ceremonially, the Table therefore might be prepared before anything begins. But then again, some have upheld the need for elders to dress and move in a specific way, with an understanding that they come at this point in the service to have something of a hierarchical role alongside the minister around the Communion Table, and this argues for a movement out of the pews to being around the table.

Those who are to move may be elders or others who will be involved in bringing up the Communion elements and/or distributing them.[35] We should note that while historically elders have guarded the discipline of the Table,[36] it has not necessarily been the case that they have a particular role to assist in the distribution, in that when all the people would sit around tables, it was regarded as essential that each should serve the other. In the now common situation of people being served in their pews or ordinary seats, duty elders may again be visible but always so as to enable the participation of all. There may be

35 Children might be an example, expressing the conviction that such as these are an equal and an important part of the worshipping community. There may be others also whose presence would be noticed and add significance to the action. At York Minster, for instance, two visitors are identified at the start of the service and invited to join the procession sharing the carrying of the Communion vessels.

36 In some places, there has arisen the tradition of constituting the Kirk Session when the Sacrament is celebrated: this is neither necessary nor helpful, in that the worship offered is not that of the Session alone any more than it is of the minister alone.

good grounds for questioning the allocation of particular seats[37] close to an altar-type Table if the rest of the congregation is relegated to being further away. The unfortunate practical consequence of such an arrangement is that those closest to the Table seem to be apart from the rest when the Communion meal is served. Some care will need to be taken on how to organise the distribution (see further below, section 28).

Finally, where are the bread and wine placed? If practical considerations often lead, perhaps we might stop to consider the care and precision on this demonstrated in other parts of the church catholic.

C. The sacred meal is being prepared, and we need therefore to take a step back to discern what is at the heart of the tradition – aside from what is purely practical or enshrined in (comparatively recent) memory. The people's attention is to be shifted to gathering around the Table, as opposed to sitting under the Word. Physical movement is bound to be part of this, at the very least on the part of the minister, but if not everyone is going to move, there should be others nearby, so as to express the sense of the community joining together for the meal. However, if the whole congregation is not going to move, there should be an effort also to express the links between those who are visibly up front and the rest; and a procession through the midst of the congregation might do that, joined together with a psalm or hymn for all to sing (and the music itself will set a certain tone).[38] This would be followed closely by some inclusive words (see sections 20–1 below)

37 In some places, architectural style recalls cathedral arrangements of an Episcopal throne surrounded by stalls for the presbyters. But this supported notions of concelebration by those who were ordained, as opposed to the whole community of the baptised. The borrowing therefore of such architecture issues a confusing sign in the light of our Reformed theology of worship.

38 In this way of thinking, it would be hard to justify a special dress code for those coming up to the front alongside the minister. There are some general remarks on the significance of space above, in the opening section on the minister and people coming together for worship.

and good planning of the distribution. At the same time, where numbers are small, there might be a great deal more informality. Whether the elements are laid on the Table in advance or not, they should be as visible as possible to all present (not hidden behind a table lectern, therefore!). In all that happens, it matters that the signs being given should be expressive and effective. The more our sacramental signs are understood, the more fully we can recognise the grace being conveyed.

'I come with joy, a child of God' (*CH4*, no. 656)

QUESTION FOR DISCUSSION

Are we careful to justify our rituals and our organisation of space?

20 The Grace

The minister says:

The grace of the Lord Jesus Christ be with you.

Amen.

21 The Unveiling of the Elements

The minister unveils the elements, and while doing so may say:

Let us pray.

O God,
by the blood of your dear Son,
you have consecrated for us a new and living way
into the holiest of all.
Assure us of your mercy,
and sanctify us by your heavenly grace;
that we, approaching you with pure heart
and cleansed conscience,
may offer you a sacrifice in righteousness;
through Jesus Christ our Lord.

Amen.

Out of the fullness of your gifts, O God,
we make our offerings to you,
and present this bread and this wine at your table;
for all things come from you,
and of your own do we give you.
Blessed be your holy name for ever;
through Jesus Christ our Lord.
Amen.

A. The saying at this point of the greeting from 2 Corinthians 13:13 (preferably not truncated, as here in *Common Order*?) carries a certain weight. As we are opened to the fullness of God's grace, a new set of possibilities arise in our worship and discipleship. Through grace to be received in the sharing of this bread and wine, our fellowship with one another and with the Triune God is to be deepened (see also 1 John 1:3).[39] The saying of further prayers, perhaps together with an unveiling of the elements, underlines the sense of how Christ's self-offering is to meet up with anything that we may offer. First, we confess that our entry point into *Holy* Communion depends entirely on Christ's death on the cross. In him alone are we 'pure' and 'cleansed' and justified in participating in a sacrifice of praise. Then we dedicate our offering, recognising even there that God is the provider of all that we have.

B. The Communion meal will carry very special significance, but these prayers give a hint at its outset that it is in a sense one feast among many; that God has richly provided for all of our living. At the moment that we are all set for sacramental communion of the highest order – for entry

39 It might be noted that in some other Churches, there is alternatively a sharing of the Peace – this drawing from the position suggested by the injunction in Matthew 5:23–4 to make peace with your brother / sister before coming to the altar; this will come below at section 29.

as it were into the kingdom of God – we recollect also that we owe humble thanks for the material gifts of creation. If there is a conspicuous unveiling at this point, it may be allowed so as to express, in the practical taking off of covers, something here about the sacredness of life in ordinary. What is revealed is nothing so very unusual! Yet we are to see more than we take so often for granted. Bread and wine (and money, and whatever) are signs of God's gracious providing, divine generosity which exceeds indeed more than we can ever handle. God's name is to be blessed for all good gifts: in the harvest and in every ordinary meal, in the making of money and in every aspect of human flourishing, thank-offerings will always be fitting.[40] And here and now, the bountifulness of God in creation and the highest achievements of humanity in stewarding what has been given will be very particularly focused: this ritual around bread and wine derives its meaning from Christ's last supper and from his death and resurrection.

C. The prayers are optional, and some prefer not even to have the bread and wine veiled, reckoning that their visual effectiveness speaks for itself from the outset. Or the unveiling might be done wordlessly and without panoply. The full liturgy simply points words to signal how God is source and origin of all that we do and also how our meeting-point is very much in terms of the material realities of this world. Alternative prayers might indeed encourage active participation by the whole gathered assembly.[41]

As far as the elements are concerned, the logic would be to use bread and wine that is not out of the ordinary, but then some debate has ensued. Is there a significance in using unleavened bread, given the Passover context of the Last Supper? What wine is to be used in a country

40 A. Schmemann, *For the life of the world* (St Vladimir's Press, 1970), expounds at length the significance of every meal. See too John Paul II in the Encyclical *Ecclesia de Eucharistia* (para. 8: 'the world which came forth from the hands of God the creator returns to him redeemed by Christ').

41 For example, 'Blessed are you, Lord, God of all creation . . .' which has a recurring refrain, '***Blessed be God for ever***': *Common Order*, p. 191.

like our own? Some parishes have used unleavened bread; a derivation of this, a kind of shortbread, was widely used up until the beginning of the nineteenth century, baked in thin round cakes, sometimes stamped with a cross. It would seem that water sometimes was used when wine was not available, but generally claret was used, until it was replaced by port which became popular as trade opened up after 1707. In the late nineteenth and early twentieth centuries, under the influence of the temperance movement, unfermented wine became common. Pastoral sensitivity may continue this practice, just as might be taken into consideration the awareness today of such conditions as wheat allergies. Is it appropriate to have a variety of provision? There will be an emphasis on sharing in the one bread, drinking of the one cup; if there are dietary issues, perhaps we might make it clear that it is possible for example to communicate in 'one kind' only.[42] Close by all of this area of discussion are questions of quantity and presentation. What are the appropriate vessels on which to present the bread and wine? Are they to be out of the ordinary or not?[43] A debate over hygiene comes into play also.[44]

42 Historically, there were justifiable struggles to assert a right for all God's people to take both the bread and the cup, since Christ had enjoined as much. Still, however, there would be no sense of mathematically halving the benefits of the Communion between the bread and the cup. If the body would be poisoned by the consumption of wheat or alcohol, then we scarcely bring honour to God.

43 Kirkpatrick Dobie is currently engaged in a survey of Communion plate. In 1617, an Act was passed saying that Communion was to be celebrated from vessels made from precious metal. See his unpublished essay, 'Distribution of the elements'.

44 At the turn of the nineteenth and twentieth centuries in the USA, concern about hygiene led to a proposal that individual glasses be substituted and this practice spread. The General Assembly agreed to allow their use but it remains law that the common cup shall always be available for those who wish it. On the hygiene question the Panel on Worship has invited medical opinion and a report on this is within the CD-ROM material. In sum: the conclusion was that no published cases of cross-infection from the use of the common cup had been recorded. It acknowledges the possibility of a greater risk in a crowded church. Microbiologists say that there is a poorly defined but nonetheless possible risk

And how much bread and wine should be laid out? How much will be consumed? There have been historical variations in how much people are prepared to eat and drink in the context of the Lord's Supper,[45] before even getting to the question of how appropriately to dispose of what has not been consumed. There are strong arguments that just as we are to be moved away from taking any food or material blessings for granted, so we are not to waste what is set before us, especially when there are others who go unfed. There are points here we shall return to.

'Here, O my Lord, I see thee face to face' (*CH4*, no. 664)

QUESTION FOR DISCUSSION

How will we hold together the ordinary and the extra-ordinariness of the Communion event?

of cross-infection. It should be borne in mind, however, that the material from which cups are made is not the most hospitable surface for microbes. Further, alcoholic wine is known to have an antibacterial function. The author's advice was to keep a sense of proportion, given the many other aspects of human contact there were, including kissing!

45 See L. E. Schmidt, *Holy Fairs*, who chronicles the nineteenth-century shift on the amount consumed in Scottish Communions.

22 Narrative of the Institution

The minister says:

Hear the words of the institution
of the Lord's Supper,
according to St Paul:
The tradition which I handed on to you
came to me from the Lord himself:
that on the night of his arrest
the Lord Jesus took bread,
and after giving thanks to God
broke it and said:
'This is my body, which is for you;
do this in memory of me.'
In the same way, he took the cup after supper,
and said:
'This cup is the new covenant
sealed by my blood.
Whenever you drink it, do this in memory of me.'
For every time you eat this bread
and drink the cup,
you proclaim the death of the Lord,
until he comes.

1 Corinthians 11:23–6

A. This section used to be called 'the Warrant', in that Reformed theology laid emphasis on the Scriptural basis of the Sacrament and its institution by Christ himself.[46] That said, it may be stretching a point to say that it

46 This is explicit in the Genevan order brought to Scotland in 1559, the first *Book of Discipline*, the first *Book of Common Order* and so on. In the *Westminster Directory*, where liturgical points are pared to a minimum, still it is there!

is the Last Supper alone that is the basis for the Sacrament. The 'Lord's Supper' and the 'Last Supper' perhaps become confused in people's minds. Probably we should be thinking also of something building on the succession of meals Jesus had with his followers, not least the Resurrection meals – the breakfast on the beach, the meal behind locked doors, the supper at Emmaus. For the church's regular patterning of its life, there were probably also influences from the society in the context of which the new faith was evolving its rituals; attention has been drawn to a development within the Hellenistic *polis*, where one symbol of the responsibilities and belonging ('koinonia', Greek for 'communion' or 'fellowship') of members was a common meal incorporating an ethical programme, often with a religious dimension.[47] In any case, it is possible just in the pages of Scripture to see the evolving form of the Sacrament. If we read 1 Corinthians alongside the four Gospels, or take then the Didache,[48] all have different orders for the event – the meal with the cup following, the cup before the bread, bread and cup together; evidence for separation between real meals and sacramental actions. Scholars warn against seeing church practice evolving seamlessly. It seems, instead, that for the first few centuries there was great variety of ritual act and indeed of the significance attached to these acts, and the belief of such scholars as Gregory Dix in a standardisation of practice from earliest times is misplaced.[49] Even Dix's famous 'fourfold shape' (taking, blessing, breaking the bread, sharing), which he believed was derived from a sevenfold shape allegedly present in accounts of the Last Supper, is not any longer found helpful. Also, the widely accepted view that the great thanksgiving prayer developed from the Jewish *berakah* is now questioned.

And yet, this all said, in most early liturgies, once they had become established, and at least by the fourth century, the institution narrative

47 See Nicholas Sagovsky, *Ecumenism, Christian Origins and the Practice of Communion* (Cambridge UP, 2000), pp. 48ff., and John Reumann in Best and Gassmann (eds), *On the Way to Fuller Koinonia*, pp. 40–1.

48 *The Didache* dates from the second century.

49 See Paul Bradshaw, *Eucharistic Origins* (SPCK, 2004).

was part of the great thanksgiving prayer (where it continues in other main traditions). While this is an option within our liturgical published texts,[50] its placing here before the thanksgiving prayer, frames very exactly, in Scriptural, terms what is about to be done in line with holy tradition. The Lord's Supper is totally bound up with the Passion of Christ, from Last Supper through to Resurrection.

One point worth noting in the order as published is the modification in our own day from earlier authorised forms in the Reformed tradition.[51] It is up for debate whether we finish quoting the Corinthians text at v. 26 rather than at v. 27, and here we might refer back to the discussion about questions of worthiness in relation to participation (see opening section above on 'The minister and people come together'; also section 17 above).

B. The retelling of a story of faith has long been the practice of God's people, for it helps us to conceptualise who we are and where we have come from. It sends us into the future with a faith in what God has done in the past and a promise that God will continue to work our salvation. The retelling of the Last Supper and Lord's Supper stories roots us through our imagination to be connected with those who have gone before us, and shapes us for living as the church today. The Word is followed through in act, which is altogether transformational. And as the tradition lives no longer confined to the printed letter, we might be wary of unpicking the story too far. It is not for us to change a moving picture into a set of actions which must be followed exactly for fear of heresy or law.[52]

50 The 1996 reprint of *Common Order* drew attention to this possibility, and showed how adaptation might be made, while the 2005 edition gives an actual example (in the Third Order) of how it would fit with the rest of the prayer.

51 Note that the *Westminster Directory* of 1645, a historic standard for the Church of Scotland, explicitly maintained the need to read up to the 27th verse.

52 Cf. Marcus Borg, *Meeting Jesus again for the first time* (Harper, 1994), p. 120. We might pause here to consider how much and what sort of expression to use in the reading, or reciting by heart, of the Warrant.

The riches of the Last Supper memory come in the connections to be made with the Passover meal, for all that the Gospels are not entirely agreed whether Jesus and his friends ate on a Thursday or a Friday. The community of the Old Covenant is one that is now new in Christ; his blood replaces the sacrifice of the lamb. There is a moment of definitive revelation. Table fellowship as Jesus lived it is hugely important. His death on the cross seals the good news of our being forgiven and called into new horizons of hope. And yet still there is a tension between the 'now' and the 'not yet'. We wait for Christ coming again. In the context of 1 Corinthians, the words of the institution are taught as a corrective to bad practice within a community where there were factions and self-indulgence. That the tradition to be adhered to is to call us into good practice, honouring Christ as he lived and died.

C. We would be unwise in any sense to leave behind this core story of the institution of the Lord's Supper. The salvation of God is rooted in Scripture, Old and New Testaments; fellowship as a community of the forgiven is our essential calling. However, there is room for questioning whether anything is bound to happen simply through the recitation of the words by a certain person, just as we might be cautious of precisely defining, to the satisfaction only of some, all the meaning that is here contained. Historically, there is a lot of baggage here. However, in that the narrative shapes the space in which we share the bread and wine, while there may be value in exploring sometimes other ways into the space – a variety of words and stories, perhaps drama, mime, song – the 1 Corinthians narrative will still be used frequently (most often!), lest we forget and move away from the tradition. But let us be clear that what is handed on is ours so that we might live. The Warrant being recited, say, by someone in the worshipping community who has acutely experienced alienation or estrangement from justice may encourage a powerful hearing in new light. The imaginations of all those who will respond, of all ages and backgrounds, are to be stirred.[53] This is not

53 Roddy Hamilton in his essay entitled 'Narrative of the Institution', on the CD-ROM, helpfully offers some creative story forms to ponder if not to use.

a text for routinely droning through. It is more than just a piece in a liturgical jigsaw.

'Now, my tongue, the mystery telling of the glorious body sing' (*CH4*, no. 667)

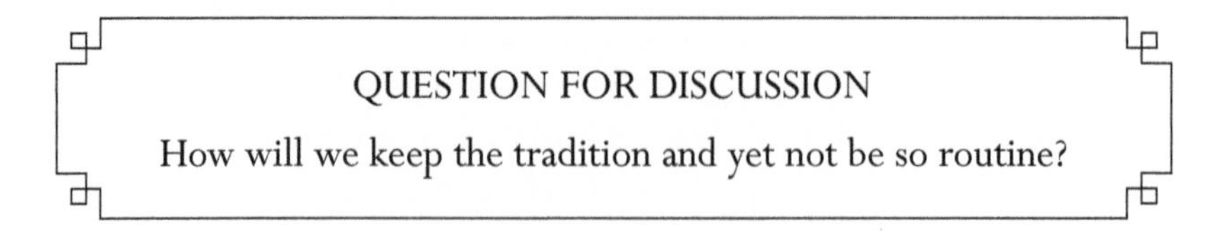

23 Taking of the Bread and Wine

The minister says:

As the Lord Jesus,
the same night in which he was betrayed,
took bread,
I take these elements of bread and wine,
to be set apart from all common uses
to this holy use and mystery;
and as he gave thanks and blessed,
let us draw near to God
and offer him our prayers and thanksgiving.

A. The inclusion of this form of words advances the line of locating the Lord's Supper in the context of the Last Supper. Moreover, it signals the intention that the ordinary gifts of God in bread and wine here will assume a very special signification: they will be set apart for the sacramental sharing. If the words of the institution may be said by any member of the gathered community, these now are words belonging to the one who presides by virtue of ordination. He or she will lead the community in prayers so as to join the whole company in the spirit of Christ.

B. This text therefore introduces the notion of consecration. Such an act is not tied down to particular words and gestures, nor to the voice of one set apart, although there is certainly meaning and value there. Rather, it is both the intention and the completeness of the proceedings, and the openness to the moving of the Holy Spirit, which will achieve the desired end. There is a sense in which the entire liturgy is a single piece, with no one part exalted above another. We will act in accordance with the tradition; and God in His grace will respond, according to promise. What is holy is of God, not of ourselves.[54] Note also in all of this that the prayers and thanksgivings to be offered are of the whole community, and not of the presiding minister alone. All that follows is addressed to God by all together.[55]

C. One question which has troubled the church is the discernment of where holiness begins and ends. In the light of deep and far-ranging historical controversies, to say as little as is here is but a beginning on this subject. Most obviously we should take note of the keen debate over the material elements of the Lord's Supper, with concern in some quarters over every visible particle of the bread and wine. Reformed theology, taking a significant lead from the thought of John Calvin, has resisted signing up to the distinctions based on Aristotelian science, preferring rather to dwell literally on the action of the Supper being 'holy use and mystery'. Thus, the use implies participation by the assembled company, with all together receiving from Christ. The one ordained to preside has a key representational, even priestly role, but does not as it were possess any power other than to lead the prayers and to be a keeper of good order. For the Sacrament, it is Christ who gives himself to us, and that is best summed up by the notion of mystery ('mysterion' in the Greek being the term which in Latinisation became 'sacrament', *sacramentum).*[56]

54 See A. Schmemann, *The Eucharist* (St Vladimir's Press,1987), pp. 13–14, for a critique of the tendency to single out particular moments in the liturgy, and the argument, which the Reformers would recognise, that the church is constituted by worship.

55 Liturgy etymologically links the people ('*laos*') and action or service. The one who presides prays to God on behalf of all who are gathered. See Giraudo, 'The Eucharist as *Diakonia*', p. 128.

56 Cf. especially the letter to the Ephesians. While '*sacramentum*' is not a direct translation of '*mysterion*', its Latin roots which connect it with the making and keeping of an oath or solemn promise adds to the sense in which God is the initiator of what is happening.

The sovereignty of God thus is deeply respected and, in particular, the freedom of the Holy Spirit. This does not diminish belief in there being a 'real Presence', as has sometimes been thought, but it holds back from too precisely timing it or tying it down.[57] However, in all the ecumenical exchanges, latterly thankfully in more peaceful mode than in former generations, it has become clear that Christians in our tradition are more likely to be attracted to reductionism in some mode or other, i.e. seeing the Lord's Supper as more a human act than an occasion for God's close encounter; *Common Order*, in line with all the historic Reformed standards, would clearly resist this. We believe in Holy Communion.

Nevertheless, there is a question left rather unaddressed which connects here, namely what we do with bread and wine left over from the Supper. Might this be shared significantly with those who for reasons of poor health, say, have been unable to gather with the full assembly? And if it cannot all be so used, is it not a sign of reverence for the mystery that among those present the remainder be consumed and certainly not just casually jettisoned? To this we shall return.

'Let all mortal flesh keep silence' (*CH4*, no. 666)

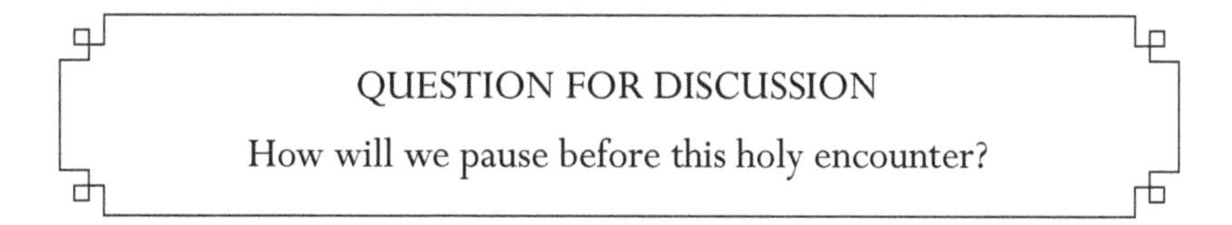

57 Calvin is very close to Aquinas in his reading of sacramental, as opposed to spatial, presence – John E. Colwell, *Promise and Presence* (Paternoster, 2005), pp. 167–71. One salient question is whether we anticipate Christ coming down to meet us at the table, or whether we are raised in our hearts to feast with him in the heavenly places. Much of Reformed tradition would follow the Orthodox emphasis, i.e. on the latter. Cf. Schmemann, *The Eucharist*, passim.

24 Thanksgiving

It is the giving of thanks to the creator, redeemer and sustainer that is most characteristic of the relationship between God and humankind. While debates continue to trouble the church as to how the Lord's Supper or Eucharist or Mass works, the note of thanksgiving (in the Greek, *eucharistia*)[58] is commonly and profoundly a point of sharing. As we meet with and are met by Christ, we are thankful! It is then regrettable that the great prayer of thanksgiving can be thought of as a bit of a marathon, something to put up with, for in fact it is a very meaningful few minutes. One of the liturgy's greatest dramas cannot and must not be clouded by it feeling like a tedious, ministerial monologue. Therefore, the way we handle it is important and it requires all our skills of pace and timing.

This first order offers three options for prayers. The first follows a classical pattern in structure and language, which we shall mainly focus on here.[59] The point is to discern how this form of prayer brings out certain key themes at the heart of our Communion celebrations. As has already been noted, there is no perfect form of the Eucharistic prayer continuously used since the church began. The historical evidence seems to show that prayers used were a conjunction of discrete units, probably uttered extempore according to local convention before becoming more regulated for the sake of public and formal events. There may still be

58 The word Eucharist as a title for the meal has been applied since the second century, in the first Apology of Justin Martyr. See Justin, *Prima Apologia*, 67, 5, quoted in Giraudo, 'The Eucharist as *Diakonia*', p. 103.

59 The second is from the *Genevan Service Book*, which formed the basis for the first (sixteenth-century) *Book of Common Order*. The third is one of the common texts agreed through the English Language Liturgical Consultation (ELLC).

flexibility – though we would do well to note Calvin's good arguments for agreed forms: first, to help 'the unskilfulness and simplicity of some'; second to maintain harmony between the churches; thirdly, so that 'a capricious giddiness and levity of such as effect innovations may be prevented'.[60]

The minister says:

The Lord be with you.
And also with you.

Lift up your hearts.
We lift them to the Lord.

Let us give thanks to the Lord our God.
It is right to give our thanks and praise.

A. This introductory dialogue, known historically from its Latin version as the *Sursum corda*, appears very early in the development of the Eucharistic prayer. It serves to establish the thanksgiving as a communal utterance rather than a purely ministerial effort. In effect, the president is receiving from the assembly the authority to give thanks in the name of all. Further than that, the minister, as the one ordained to the role within the worshipping congregation, draws the gathered people towards appreciating the presence of Christ, in whom we offer all our worship.[61]

60 J. Calvin, *Opera Quae Supersunt Omnia*, volume xiii, p. 70. The remarks echo words issued over a millennium earlier by Theodore of Mopsuestia. See Giraudo, 'The Eucharist as *Diakonia*', p. 129. The CD-ROM material offers some contemporary and very different thanksgiving liturgies for consideration.

61 Cf. Psalm 22:22, 25–6, a famously Messianic text. The origins of the words themselves have been variously traced, both in early liturgical material and in Scripture itself: Wainwright et al, *The Study of Liturgy*, p. 190, n. 6. The tradition of adding gesture to this prayer would have the president raising arms at 'lift up

It is a great pity that notwithstanding the printing of this as a dialogue as early as the Church of Scotland's *Prayers for Divine Service* in 1923, and its inclusion in *CH3* at no. 559 (and now in *CH4* at no. 650), few congregations habitually respond out loud. Without a response, the dialogue can only convert to a conversation with self, unless only the first line is said in each case. It is to be hoped that the recent publishing of the CD-ROM of our worship books will make it easy to print this and other material in an order of service.

a. It is indeed right, it is our duty and our joy,
at all times and in all places,
to give you thanks and praise,
holy Father, heavenly King,
almighty and eternal God.

We give thanks
that in the creation of the world,
when you laid the earth's foundation
and set its corner-stone in place,
the morning stars sang in chorus
and the angels of God all shouted for joy.
By the power of your Spirit,
you made the universe;
by the might of your Word,
you gave us life.

We give thanks
that in the new creation,
when you gave your Son to raise us up again,
since we and all our human race had fallen,
you claimed us for your own people;

---

your hearts', in a gesture of lifting. The arms might then be kept lifted until the end of the 'Holy, holy ...'; dropping them after this point also marks the slight change of key thereafter, where the note of receiving becomes strong.

that we might proclaim the glorious deeds
of him who has called us out of darkness
into his marvellous light.
By the life of your Spirit,
you fill the hearts of the faithful;
by the light of your Word,
you give us strength and love.

This is the 'Preface', Latin *praefatio*, meaning not 'preliminary' but 'proclamation'. Here is declared the foundation for the expression of thankfulness which is the heart of this prayer, and the whole action of Communion. The giving of thanks in this way echoes Jesus' own prayers over meals (e.g. Mark 8:6 and accounts of Last Supper). This ringing recital of the whole history of salvation is in the kind of elevated, metaphorical language designed not so much to state doctrine as to call forth an answering emotion on the part of the worshipper, the emotion of awe and gladness, not just as a state of mind but as something that motivates the will. A number of significant themes sound in this foundational thanksgiving. Creation and the new creation are linked together, sin and redemption, the Spirit and the Son. The faithfulness of God's people will surely spill out of the sanctuary.

Here may be added the Proper Preface (pp. 185 to 189)

The general 'proclamation' applies whenever Christians gather, but the different parts of the Christian year have different emphases or shades. In the East, (a version of) this preface was reiterated week by week, but in the West the different seasons brought out particular prefaces appropriate (= 'proper') to the time of the Christian year. Today we have the best of both worlds, with the 'proper preface' added to the 'ordinary' preface, this 'customising' of the celebration given a splash of seasonal colour. The distinction between 'ordinary' and 'proper' applies also over the whole action of the Holy Communion, in that there are prayers we will use again and again, whenever we gather.[62] But the proper preface is more than just adding a bit of variety. The Christian Year is a hallowing of human time. God's time and human time, by God's grace, are allowed to overlap. In the pattern of the year we are enabled to move in and out of God's time so that the mighty events of our salvation are marrying with our fragmented and fragile time frame.

Therefore, with your people
of all places and times,
and with the whole company of heaven,
we proclaim your greatness
and sing your praise in the angels' song:

> ***Holy, holy, holy Lord,***
> ***God of power and might,***
> ***heaven and earth are full of your glory.***
> ***Hosanna in the highest.***
> ***Blessed is he who comes***
> ***in the name of the Lord.***
> ***Hosanna in the highest.***

Here a certain climax is reached, and again we are reminded that this is not an act of the priest or minister, but a celebration in the hands of the whole gathered people. Indeed, the reference to the company of heaven recognises most appropriately at this point that God's praises are sung not only by human tongues. Together everyone says or sings: 'Holy, holy, holy Lord ...', an ancient 'ordinary' hymn known also as the *Sanctus*. This is followed by the 'Blessed is he who comes'. Both texts are deeply Scriptural, reflecting Isaiah 6/Revelation 4:8, and

62 The 'ordinary' prayers run from beginning through to the end: the 'Kyrie' / Lord, have mercy, the 'Gloria' / Glory to God in the highest, the Creed, the 'Sanctus et Benedictus' / Holy, holy and Blessed is he, and the Agnus Dei / Lamb of God. In practice, musical settings can be used.

Matthew 21:9, etc. (the entry into Jerusalem, which in turn reflects Psalm 118).[63] There is a strong argument for everyone to join in. This Eucharistic prayer is in no sense meant to be presented didactically: it requires participation and the more this can be signalled, the better.

Just as the singing of prayers from ancient times was reckoned to be an expression of reverent worship, it is entirely appropriate that the congregation join together in singing at this point, and there are many simple settings that can be picked up.

In tune with all the heavenly hosts,
we here on earth acknowledge your glory,
and give you thanks that in the fullness of time
you sent your Son to be our Saviour.

We bless you
for his incarnation among us,
his holy birth,
his perfect life on earth,
his suffering for us, and his triumph over death;
for his ascension to your right hand
and his gift of the Holy Spirit;
and for the promise of his coming again.

Remembering his work and passion,
and pleading his eternal sacrifice,
we follow his example and obey his command.

Now there is a change of pitch. Beyond the shout of thanksgiving, perhaps with hands raised and voices joined in song, the prayer here takes on a greater intensity as it visits God's act in sending Jesus Christ.

63 Their origins in the Eucharistic prayer are obscure – Jewish-Christian? Syrian? – though they have been in regular use since the fourth century. In many older liturgies, Catholic and Reformed, the cherubim and seraphim of Isaiah 6 would be explicitly named; to be in company just 'with the angels' is a toning down of the reality!

We are blessed by who he was and what he has done for us, and there is a series of creed-like affirmations. But ultimately, the key word in this section is 'Remembering', and there more is intended than a recall; the sense is that this is about renewal even here and now. Technically this is '*anamnesis*', which is to say that the great act of redemption of days past is almost being replayed in the contemporary setting; certainly we have an experience of it, as 'we follow his example and obey his command', entering as it were the heavenly realm. The momentous sacrifice at Calvary has eternal force, crossing time and space, as indeed all that Jesus Christ was and is. Jesus continues to intercede for us.[64] Therefore as we believe in Communion, we are bound not to distant memory, but rather to the church together with its Lord, on earth as it is in heaven. This is a key and awesome moment of anticipation.

If, as is allowed for in the reprints of *Common Order*, there is now also explicit reference to the institution narrative of 1 Corinthians 11, this further locks our vision into place. What was long ago ordained carries into our contemporary celebration. He shares his very life with us. He has poured out his life for us. This is our food and this is our drink. It is to be digested, for we are to understand that our being alive depends on it. We are alive to God through him.

> Send down your Holy Spirit
> to bless us
> and these your gifts of bread and wine,
> that the bread which we break
> may be for us the communion
> of the body of Christ,
> and the cup of blessing which we bless

64 Cf. World Council of Churches, *Baptism, Eucharist and Ministry*, 'Eucharist', pp. 5–10; also Colwell, *Promise and Presence*, pp. 155–61, who argues powerfully for there being closer agreement than is sometimes appreciated between Reformed and Roman Catholic thought in this area. There is 'commemorative representation' of the once for all sacrifice on Calvary. See also John Paul II, *Ecclesia de Eucharistia*, paras 12–14.

the communion of the blood of Christ;
that we, receiving them,
by faith may be made partakers
of his body and blood,
with all his benefits,
to nourish us
and help us grow in grace,
to the glory of your most holy name.

Here is another deeply significant moment in the prayers. As soon as Christ's presence is so deeply reverenced, the role of the Holy Spirit is explicitly invoked. Blessing of the Holy Spirit is asked upon those who participate and upon the gifts of bread and wine and upon the action about to be fulfilled – yet again the intention and completeness of the celebration being upheld. If we resist a 'magical' moment in the use of the words of the institution, so also we would hold back from assigning overwhelming significance to this part of the prayer, the 'epiclesis' as it is called. The sovereignty of God must be respected. And yet when the epiclesis was omitted from Knox's earliest forms of prayers, this was a bone of contention even at the time – though the probable reasoning for the omission was that desire to avoid any suggestion that simply a formula would achieve a change in the bread and wine; Knox still invoked the Spirit's help upon the communicants (before the Eucharistic prayers began). The recovery of the form preserved more consistently in the Eastern churches than in the West is agreed to be most valuable, lest we impoverish the doctrine of the Trinity.[65] Calvin

65 As with other parts of the Eucharistic prayers, the earliest sources are less easy to tie down, but the epiclesis was well established by the fourth or fifth centuries, but in the Roman rite say of the eighth century it had disappeared. Since Vatican II, the epiclesis has been reinstated, but in Roman liturgy prior to the words of institution (cf. *Book of Common Prayer* of Edward VI, 1549). See M. Thurian, 'The Lima Liturgy' in Best and Heller, *Eucharistic Worship*, pp. 18–19. For a critical

of course insisted that the Holy Spirit was critical to accomplishing what was signified.

And here we offer and present to you
our very selves,
to be a living sacrifice,
dedicated and fit for your acceptance;
through Jesus Christ our Lord.

Faith anticipates the presence of the Christ who saves and the Spirit who sanctifies, and here, in language picking up appropriately from the letter to the Romans (ch. 12), faith on the part of those present is affirmed to be living and active. We will offer ourselves in response to what Christ has done for us. Our self-offering is held within his sacrificial work. And worship implies the commitment of body and soul. There is a material and spiritual wholeness, not only in what there is for us to receive, but in what is ours to give. This is a serious and sobering point, for that word 'sacrifice' is not used lightly, certainly neither of Christ, nor of ourselves. As Bonhoeffer so famously wrote, there is a cost to discipleship.

[Brief remembrance may be made here of matters and people that lie close to the worshippers' hearts, each petition beginning, 'Remember, O Lord, ...' (see p. 163).]

It was at this point that in ancient practice the *diptychs* would be inserted, commemorative intercessions referring both to the living

---

perspective, resisting an emphasis on the epiclesis, see Donald Macleod, 'Calvin into Hippolytus?' in Spinks and Torrance, *To glorify God*, pp. 263–7. Finally, whereas some might argue for a gesture at this point, contributing to people's reception of and openness towards the Spirit's presence, this is not beyond argument, lest it overwrite the significance of this part of the prayer and the power within the person who utters it.

and the departed (the word means 'double-folded' – two lists), and intense, given the special place that they are being uttered. Although *Common Order* inclines to suggest this may not be the norm,[66] there is something precious here. Not only does it hold together thanksgiving and intercession, as often in Scripture, but also it expands the horizons beyond those present to all who are absent, yet still part of Christ's transforming work. Reference will be made, therefore, very naturally both to the living and the departed. While the Reformed church frowned most severely on prayers for the dead, rejecting the doctrine of purgatory, the tradition here is much older and centred around the expectation very much owned in the Reformed Confessions of the unity of the faithful at the end of time; early liturgical sources push us towards maintaining a strong eschatological dimension, though the principal emphasis would still rest on those who are 'pilgrims below'. It is noteworthy that surviving forms of such prayers emphasise a width of concern and care for the church which gathers to meet Christ at his table on earth. Do our horizons of God's saving purposes too readily reduce to the people we see and worship with?

Through him, with him, in him,
in the unity of the Holy Spirit,
all honour and glory are yours,
almighty Father, now and for ever.
Amen.

The closing doxology is intended to be said by all present. Its terms derive from ancient forms of singing praise. While it is in itself rich,

66 Only the Third Order contains an example of this with its short utterances at the end of the thanksgiving prayer all beginning 'Remember, O Lord ...' See also the 'Shorter Order' of the 1940 book and the second order of the 1979 book. Historically the early Scottish Reformed texts were no different, following the new line taken in the second Edwardian Prayer Book of 1552. Some early texts are quoted in Peter Donald's essay, 'Intercessions and more', on the CD-ROM.

what is desirable, at the very least, is that the people should join in the closing 'Amen'. For this great prayer, from start to finish, has asked for their participation.

B. In our tradition we do not lay down rigorously what words must be used. This is not just to avoid the superstitious belief that certain formulae 'effect' certain conditions, but arises from the understanding that Christ is present and his grace is proffered whether or not we invent liturgies, even though these forms of words and actions are our necessary way of articulating, receiving and responding to Christ's initiative in reaching out to us. We are 'dipping into' a reality that pre-exists us and our formulations. What we hope to enable in our celebration of Holy Communion is a fullness of encounter between the Body and the Head. This encounter is many-sided and the historical development of worship and doctrine offers both to capture and release the truth for each new generation. We ought to ally words to signs so that they may connect them and us to the central things they represent, thus to awaken the assembly anew to their significance and to draw in their most complete participation. The length of the First Order is not to do with putting everything in so much as pacing the event to the majesty of the encounter when it is a main celebration on a Sunday morning. Study of the other orders in the book show that completeness can also come with greater brevity, but completeness there should be.

C. The first order thus offers a form which both defines and opens up to the mystery. The sacramental moment is extended, neither captured by particular words nor by a particular actor, dependent rather on Christ coming himself into our midst as we, two or three, are gathered together in his name. Nevertheless the presidency of the one ordained to a ministry of Word and Sacrament and a faithfulness to the full riches of the tradition – in whatever words are offered – are not incidental. It is not for us just to make it up, just to be creative on the hoof, so to speak. We enter here into a communion not only with those who are present, but with all those who have gathered in all times and in all places, and we trust to be one together in Christ our Lord.

'*Father most loving, listen to your children*' (*CH4*, no. 657)

QUESTION FOR DISCUSSION

How will we pray our thanksgivings?

25 The Lord's Prayer

Our Father in heaven,
hallowed be your name,
your kingdom come,
your will be done,
on earth as in heaven.
Give us today our daily bread.
Forgive us our sins
as we forgive those who sin against us.
Save us from the time of trial
and deliver us from evil.
For the kingdom, the power,
and the glory are yours now and forever.
Amen.

A. To say or sing together the Lord's Prayer comes as a moment of simplicity after the very developed thanksgiving prayer. There is something reassuringly ordinary here, and in content of course the direction is very forward-looking. Just as at no point can the Communion service be a tired repetition of stale, outdated practices, so the tenor of the Lord's Prayer insists that the would-be followers of Jesus Christ look forward in hope. If we feel overfamiliar with it, perhaps we might recall how in the past it was reserved for the knowledge only of those who would enter in on the sacred mysteries, i.e. not outsiders to the life of the church. It is hugely meaningful!

B. The version printed here is that published in 1988 by the English Language Liturgical Consultation, a body on which the Church of

Scotland is represented through the Joint Liturgical Group of Great Britain.[67] Members of the Church of Scotland are and have in the past been involved in person in the work of ELLC. The purpose of the 'new' texts (actually revisions of the work of the International Consultation on Common Texts of 1970–5) was to have a set of texts in good contemporary language which could be found in use in all English-speaking worship assemblies. By way of calling the Church's attention to them, these are the versions printed in *Common Order* (with the new version of the Lord's Prayer offered as the first option, although the older version is also printed). Ministers and Kirk Sessions will make their own decisions about whether to use the old or new version, or indeed to employ them both in different contexts.

C. The essentials of prayer are defined by Jesus Christ himself. The essentials of discipleship refer to him. In saying the Lord's Prayer we join in a tradition with all other Christians. Our worship is complete through him, in him, in the unity of the Holy Spirit. He is our Light, our Salvation.

'Our Father' (*CH4*, no. 652)

QUESTION FOR DISCUSSION

Can we linger on and love this prayer for all that we may feel that we know it so well?

67 In respect of the Lord's Prayer, some branches of the Church have made small alterations, but the Church of Scotland remains faithful to the agreed texts.

26 Breaking of bread

The minister may hold up the bread and wine, and say:

Holy things of God for the holy people of God.

Only Jesus Christ is holy;
we are made holy in him.

The minister [returns the elements to the table, and] says:

According to the holy institution, example,
and command of our Lord Jesus Christ,
and as a memorial of him,
we do this:
who, on the night when he was betrayed,
took bread

(the minister takes the bread),

and when he had given thanks he broke it

(the minister breaks the bread),

and said, 'This is my body
which is (broken) for you;
do this in remembrance of me.'
In the same way he took the cup

(the minister [pours wine into the cup and] raises the cup)

saying, 'This cup is the new covenant
sealed by my blood.
Whenever you drink it, do it in memory of me.'

A. The exchange at the beginning of this section was not in the 1994 version of *Common Order* but was added at the reprinting two years later, drawing on ancient patterns. The words insist on the holiness of all that is present, namely the bread and wine itself and those who are present to receive – yet as soon as that is said, there is a response, which insists even more strongly that only Christ is truly holy, and that such holiness as we may talk about in this Communion event is utterly bound up with him. It is his sacramental sharing at which we are privileged guests, every one of us, and in which the bread and wine will become our spiritual food. Thus, as the Minister then proceeds to repeat once again the narrative of the institution[68] but this time with actions representing the presence of Christ, the communicants are drawn into that holy mystery by which Christ meets even now with his people. This must not be about play-acting, for the presiding Minister has not changed his or her identity; the point is to see Christ truly giving himself to us. This is more than a merely human gathering, and there is more to be received than merely bread and wine.

B. The borrowing from ancient tradition is not without its problems. The (literally!) high point in Western liturgies was when people would jostle for position the better to see, and to reverence, the elements when they were elevated. It is no surprise to know that the Reformers excised this action, fearing that the veneration of material things as if Christ was 'corporally' or 'carnally' present would give rise to superstition and idolatry.[69] As before, we shall resist this being the moment which is more

68 The careful reader, however, will note that *Common Order* inexplicably now varies the wording between 'remembrance' and 'memory'. This is both inconsistent with section 22 above, and a novelty of the 1995 book, in comparison with previous books. Perhaps there are arguments in favour of either English word (one might question indeed whether either is fully satisfactory, without explanation), but it does seem very strange to be so indecisive! One wonders whether this is a misprint!

69 The matter is explicitly mentioned in the *Westminster Confession* as 'contrary to the nature of this sacrament, and to the institution of Christ'.

loaded than any other. Yet, the Reformers were not saying that the event was one merely of symbolic value. The *Scots Confession*, while warning about worshipping the signs in place of the reality signified, insisted, with Scripture, that 'the bread which we break is the communion of Christ's body and the cup of blessing which we bless the communion of his blood'. Only 'great reverence' was therefore appropriate in the Communion event, both with regard to the participants' integrity and of how they would eat and drink.[70]

Will we then lift up the bread and the cup for all to see? There is something desirable about restoring some of the non-verbal aspects of worship, so that the senses might assist the mind to a fuller worship. The wine might be visibly poured. The bread might be dramatically broken.[71] An act of raising the elements, especially in a large building, might help to focus the action that is taking place, allowing the visual component to match the verbal. For what is done at the one table is most certainly not a private matter for the minister and elders who are closest by.

C. It is notable that in *Common Order*, there are no alternative wordings for the breaking of bread, which is not the case in other liturgical material, even within the Reformed family. This goes back to the *Westminster Directory of Worship* of 1645 which stipulated that this form should be used, so that Christ's words, or those of the apostle Paul, might precede the communion. If there appears to be repetition here, it is deliberate, for the sake of upholding this sacred mystery in which we may neither overreach ourselves, nor undersell what Christ has commanded to be done. Nevertheless, perhaps still some care is needed here, lest we focus a moment of consecration in these words

70 The point is that Christ says of the bread, 'This is my body'. It can no longer be just bread. But on the notion of transubstantiation still not being satisfactory, cf. Colwell, *Promise and Presence*, pp. 161–5.

71 Should any of the bread be cut up in advance? This is a frequent practice, but perhaps for practical reasons only, and does it obscure the sign to support the words of Christ being broken for us?

being said by a particular person. As before, the sovereignty of the Holy Spirit is to be respected.[72]

'Bread of life, hope of the world' (*CH4*, no. 663)

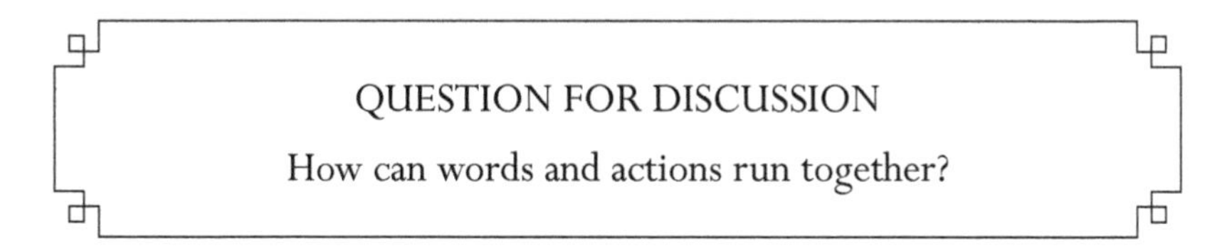

QUESTION FOR DISCUSSION

How can words and actions run together?

72 Cf. Colwell, ibid., pp. 171–5.

27 *Agnus Dei*

The minister says:

Jesus, Lamb of God,
have mercy on us.
Jesus, bearer of our sins,
have mercy on us.
Jesus, redeemer of the world,
grant us peace.

Silence may be kept for a time.

A. This tiny anthem travelled west with refugees from the Syrian (Eastern) Church in the seventh century.[73] For the Eastern Church, 'lamb' had come to mean both Christ himself and the bread of the Eucharist. This wonderful pun allied the giver of the feast with the materials used to signify his presence. We utter the exchange three times. We ask Christ's mercy and are assured that he is merciful, abounding in steadfast love, the One who forgives us and gives to us His peace. At one time the prayer was repeated for as long as it took to break sufficient bread for the people present, and its ending *grant us peace* betrays an earlier context for the sharing of the peace, in a place which corresponded to the injunction *Before coming to the table, make peace with your brother*.

B. Although the rubric suggests otherwise, this prayer is very appropriately shared in by all present. It may be said or sung, for there are many short

73 The version chosen is one of two alternative ELLC texts.

and simple musical settings (most commonly, with the older form of words). The silence provided for encourages even those who will be first to receive to take final stock of where they are and what they do.

C. In anticipation of the Communion meal, the 'benefits' are perceived, in common with the church universal. As Reformed tradition put it, 'there is no other name under heaven by which we can be saved, but the name of Jesus Christ, by whom alone we receive liberty and life, have access to the throne of grace, are admitted to eat and drink at his own table, and are sealed up by his Spirit to an assurance of happiness and everlasting life'.[74]

'Lamb of God' (*CH4*, no. 653)

QUESTION FOR DISCUSSION

How else will we be centred in Christ? How frequently will we return here?

74 This quotation from the 1645 *Westminster Directory* picks up on imagery in the Eucharistic prayers of Knox in the *Book of Common Order*. For a lovely comparative text, see the hymn of Thomas Aquinas quoted at the end of John Paul II's *Ecclesia de Eucharistia:* 'Come then, good Shepherd, bread divine, / Still show to us thy mercy sign: / Oh, feed us, still keep us thine / so we may see they glories shine / in fields of immortality. / O thou, the wisest, mightiest, best, / our present food, our future rest, / come, make us each thy chosen guest, / co-heirs of thine, and comrades blest / with saints whose dwelling is in thee.'

28 Communion

The minister partakes of the bread and wine.

The minister says:

Draw near with faith:
receive the body of our Lord Jesus Christ
which was given for you,
and his blood which was shed for you,
and feed on him in your hearts by faith,
with thanksgiving.

Taste and see that the Lord is good.
Happy are those who find refuge in him!

In giving the bread, the minister says:

Take, eat. This is the body of Christ
which is (broken) for you.
Do this, remembering him.

In giving the cup, the minister says:

This cup is the new covenant
sealed by Christ's blood
which was shed that the sins of many
might be forgiven.
Drink from it, all of you.

The elements may be taken to the people in their seats, or the people may gather round the Holy Table.

When all have received, the vessels are returned to the Holy Table and covered.

A. This is the marvellous moment when the *koinonia* of the body of Christ, the community of the Church, the priesthood of all believers, is owned and renewed. The doors of heaven are open, and our fellowship is with the Lord of life. Reconciliation – between participants, and among all the world's peoples and within the whole creation – is not a hopeless ideal, for here we have a foretaste. The words uttered urge an active participation by those who will take and eat. Christ's arms are opened wide in embrace. We cannot stand aloof.

B. The rubric in *Common Order* first describes what the minister will say and do – partaking first and then speaking the words which interpret the event. That the minister should partake first takes up both catholic and Reformed tradition, and has prevailed for most of our history, except in cases at multiple communions when another minister(s) was present. This is not a question of ministers 'pulling rank' but rather that the minister, while representing our Lord, gives the bread and wine to all, herself or himself included – in other words he/she is not taking, but receiving. The custom of elders serving the minister last may in fact draw attention to the minister in a way that the traditional pattern does not; that custom originated in the different status and position ministers were accorded among the Seceders.[75] Modern sensibilities are sometimes thought to be helped by a similar ordering, it being regarded as selfish to take first before offering to others. For words of interpretation, the original Reformed pattern was for words to be offered throughout the time of the sharing of bread and wine; the Passion narrative would sometimes have been

75 Danish patterns varied, however: W. D. Maxwell, *The Liturgical portions of the Genevan Service Book* (The Faith Press, London, 1931), pp. 207–9. It has also been suggested that changes took hold in more recent times among Victorian parlour sensitivities and courtesies. It was maintained in the service books of the United Presbyterian Church and the Free Church in the nineteenth century, but the service books produced in the Church of Scotland then and throughout the twentieth century have preferred the more ancient tradition.

read, or a selection of relevant texts. Silence was suspicious lest there should be any misapprehending of what was happening.[76]

As far as the Distribution is concerned, Reformed tradition has always been keen to emphasise the corporate aspect of the celebration. It is not for individuals to go up to an altar, or for all to receive from one person; rather the bread and the wine will be passed from hand to hand as people sit alongside one another. Some congregations still maintain the practice of therefore bringing people up literally to sit around the Table;[77] others who have the congregation seated in pews have devised routines for elders or others to assist the distribution all around the church building. It is important that this is done well, involving as many as are comfortably needed; there should be no delays in making sure that all are served. It should be as clear as possible that there are no preferential options, but that all come equally in need of Christ's grace and goodness. This undoubtedly raises question-marks over making variable provision of common cup or individual cups at one sitting, or different sorts of bread, as also it asks for care – where not everyone comes around the Table – in how the practical arrangements are set up for serving those who sit at the Table and those who sit in the pews.[78]

A final question is how much bread or wine is to be distributed. As far as we can tell, our forebears in Scotland probably ate and drank

76 In practice nowadays, complete silence is observed in many places, with music or singing elsewhere – as far as is practical.

77 The *Westminster Directory*, never repealed as a historic standard, insists that people should be at or around a table. It is a moot point whether the nineteenth-century innovation of keeping people in pews, dressed or not, truly satisfies that intention!

78 See, as before, Kirkpatrick Dobie's essay on the evidence of practical arrangements, 'Distribution of the elements' – on the CD-ROM. One of the more unusual, and not easily justifiable, methods of distribution appears to encourage a 'do it yourself' Communion, where an individual holder is clipped to pews and filled in advance with a small quantity of wine and a morsel of bread in a compartment above. The tradition always insisted on the sharing being derived from a central place as it were, receiving from our Lord as host of the feast.

rather more at the Sacrament than most of us would be used to. Latterly, for example, devices have been invented to cut bread slices of a certain size into uniform cubes. Perhaps we might question whether the most minute portions are adequate in this foretaste of the heavenly banquet, and also given our knowledge of its very early history being tied up with full meals. Certainly it matters that there is enough to go around – that is always exceptionally important – but it also matters that we keep in mind that this is a celebration, and exemplary as an experience of what it means to rejoice in community. There is a loss in making it a seriously artificial experience of eating and drinking.[79]

C. 'One bread, one body': in our ecumenical brokenness we struggle to know that visible unity into which we are called by the Lord of the church universal. We long for the day when each and every local church may rejoice in the fullness of its connections across time and space. It is scandalous also when barriers are maintained even within the local church – segregations; any indication that some are more worthy than others. Communion is the anticipation of the new heavens and the new earth. We have died to sin and been raised to life with Christ. We share in his victory over sin and death. This is our entry into unutterable joy and peace, though of course, as for Jesus at the Last Supper, there is no denying that our labour and struggle is not yet over. But for these moments – whatever the world's distractions are all around us – we are as if in the heavenly places.

79 Cf. Duncan Forrester, *Theological Fragments* (T&T Clark, 2005), pp. 117–18. 'Where Jesus is, there is life.' It has been argued that a small taste of bread speaks of the communicant being a small part of the communion of saints. However, this smacks of special pleading.

'Take and eat' (*CH4*, no. 670)

QUESTION FOR DISCUSSION

How best do we ensure that all are fed?

29 The Peace

The minister says:

The peace of the Lord Jesus Christ be with you.
Amen.

The minister may say:

On the evening of the first Easter Day,
'when the disciples were together
behind locked doors for fear,
Jesus came and stood among them.
'Peace be with you!' he said;
then he showed them his hands and his side.
On seeing the Lord,
the disciples were overjoyed.
Jesus said again, 'Peace be with you!"
In the joyful presence of our risen Lord,
let us give one another a sign of peace.

The people may greet one another with a handshake or an embrace, and say:

The peace of Christ.

A. There are a number of scriptural references to a 'holy kiss' (e.g. 1 Thessalonians 5:26, Romans 16:16, 1 Peter 5:14)[80] and this has found liturgical expression in more than one way, but here in the action of

80 See also in the *First Apology of Justin Martyr*, c. AD 150, 'Having ended the prayers, we greet one another with a kiss.'

the giving of the Peace. While some have joined it with the Offering,[81] in the light of Jesus' command to make peace before bringing a gift to the altar (cf. Matthew 5:23ff.), in *Common Order* it comes as soon as the sacramental sharing is completed. Thus it points to the commitment to heavenly peace which is at the heart of the Sacrament; it serves as *the* motif of our onward pilgrimage. The Peace was restored to modern liturgy through the Church of South India. There are two options here – one being for the Peace to be pronounced by the minister alone, and for the people to call out 'Amen'. The other is to make more of the action, and as a text there is a pregnant drawing on Christ's words from Easter evening. Peace and joy come together. This is our path and this is our assured hope.

B. The exchange of the Peace gives a very beautiful rounding off to the corporate aspect of the Sacrament. Physical contact in the Communion service is not so much an expression of human affection as an acceptance that everyone present belongs to a new order, of those who have been made holy in Jesus Christ. For 'Jew and Greek, slave and free, male and female' (cf. Galatians 3:28) it is more than a matter of mere greeting; it is certainly more than greeting those whom one already knows and feels close to. Culturally, we may feel more inclined to shake hands than to kiss. That is understandable, for the point is that whatever is done, it should be done equally to all, not with varying degrees of affection. Yet at the same time, does an ordinary handshake sufficiently point to the new creation and the transcending of all barriers? Probably not, and perhaps a special double handshake would be a satisfactory resolution, since it will feel undoubtedly awkward for many men to kiss other men (unlike in other cultural settings). Probably the minister and whoever else is sitting in a visibly prominent place should give a lead in how the Peace should be exchanged, and this should be replicated throughout the

81 Thus Orthodox liturgy; and currently, the Roman Catholic Church is considering changing to that – Benedict XVI, *Sacramentum Caritatis*, para. 49 and n. 150.

congregation, it perhaps not being practical for everyone present to greet every other person who is there on that occasion.

C. The whole of the Communion liturgy is counter-cultural, not simply this part of it. Conventions are to be challenged, tendencies to divide and classify are to be overcome. If we are very reserved, perhaps we need to break out of that; if we are very chummy with some and not with others, again this needs to be moved out from. Though some may at first find the practice of exchanging the Peace difficult, perhaps we need to ask ourselves whether in among all our familiar formality, so to speak, we have bought into a too solemn and individualistic interpretation of what the Supper is about. Minister and people together need to reflect of how Holy Communion feeds into life after the liturgy and points towards a radical reordering of society.

'Put peace into each other's hands' (*CH4*, no. 659)

QUESTION FOR DISCUSSION

How will we, as the hymn suggests, share peace 'like a treasure'?

30 Prayers

The minister says:

Let us pray.

Gracious God,
we thank you for the love
which brings us, as food from heaven,
the life of your dear Son,
and assures us that we belong
to the company of all his faithful people
in heaven and on earth.
Grant that, strengthened by this fellowship
and by the power of his Holy Spirit,
we may continue his work in the world,
until we come
to the glory of your eternal kingdom;
through the same Jesus Christ,
your Son, our Lord. ***Amen.***

Glory to God the Father,
who brought back from the dead
our Lord Jesus Christ
and crowned him with glory and honour.

Glory to God the Son,
who lives to plead our cause
at the right hand of God,
and who will come again
to make all things new.
Glory to God the Holy Spirit,

who brings us the taste
of the good Word of God
and the power of the age to come.
Amen! Praise and glory and wisdom,
thanksgiving and honour,
power and might be to our Lord for ever! ***Amen.***

31 Hymn

A. Prayers after Communion, like the exchange of the Peace, form a bridge between the high moment of the church's liturgy and the ongoing life and witness which is critical to the church's witness. There is a sense in which our Sunday worship is on the 'eighth day', since it takes us into the life beyond at the same time as marking the start of the week;[82] ordinary days are seen against the backdrop of that eternal vista. As we pray for continuing support and strength of God, we therefore are rooted in thanksgiving for what has been received and, in this form, there is a very lovely rounding off with a doxology, a song of glory couched to God the Holy Trinity and very much reflecting Eucharistic themes of the resurrected and ascended Christ who will come again, and the work of the Holy Spirit.

B. Although in this first Order the form is that the minister will lead in prayer here, it would be entirely suitable for the congregation to join

82 See Gordon Lathrop, *Holy Things* (Augsburg, 1998), who, as a Lutheran scholar, picks up on the liturgical theology of the Orthodox theologian Alexander Schmemann. Liturgy and life are to be as one – 'saints by grace must become saints by our acts and in our whole being'. J. Meyendorff, *The Orthodox Church* (St Vladimir's Press, 2nd edn, 1981), p. 175.

in these closing prayers aloud, or for there to be a range of voices involved so as to express the sense of community commitment. There are suitable forms of prayer in plenty provided elsewhere in *Common Order*.[83] There is an emphasis that the Communion meal is food for the journey, a stopping-off point but not the end of the road. Some congregations will have the pattern of more extended thanksgiving services to be held at a separate time, but whether that happens or not (with attendant opportunities for evangelism), it would be grim if we were to instantly disperse once we had eaten our fill. The fellowship continues long after the exiting from the church doors. We are bound together in the common service of the Kingdom.[84]

C. Close alongside the post-Communion prayers is the hymn of praise which in Church of Scotland tradition followed Knox's preference for Psalm 103 (*CH4*, no. 68, 'who with abundance of good things doth satisfy thy mouth');[85] but there are many other possibilities, suiting different styles of celebration or dedication. We should exit with a song in our hearts.

'We will walk with God' (*CH4*, no. 803)

QUESTION FOR DISCUSSION

How will our worship lead us to go out with a song?

83 See *Common Order, pp.* 192–4. The *Westminster Directory* put it like this: 'The minister is to give solemn thanks to God, for his rich mercy, and invaluable goodness, vouchsafed to them in that sacrament; and to entreat for pardon for the defects of the whole service, and for the gracious assistance of his good Spirit, whereby they may be enabled to walk in the strength of that grace, as becometh those who have received so great pledges of salvation.'

84 Cf. Psalm 146, where the song of praise notes so strongly God's care for those in need.

85 For Zwingli, the choice was Psalm 112.

32 Dismissal and Blessing

The minister says:

Your eyes have seen God's love;
open them to look for the glorious hope.
Your ears have heard his songs;
close them to clamour and dispute.
Your tongues have uttered his praise;
guard them to speak the truth in love.
Your hands have been raised in worship;
stretch them out to bring forth fruit for God's glory.
Your feet have walked in his courts;
direct them into light.
Your souls and bodies have been fed
by the Word of life;
serve the Lord with joy and gladness. ***Amen.***

The minister blesses the people from God.

The blessing of God almighty,
the Father, the Son, and the Holy Spirit,
be with you. ***Amen.***

A. This final section is every bit as important as the gathering that began worship. That is why it has been given 'body' at this point. The text of this dismissal is rich and yet general. What exactly is said may alternatively relate closely to the themes of the preached Word, emphasising the transition between worship and world. The Blessing is pronounced in the name of the Holy Trinity, and a sung congregational

Amen makes a fine ending (for which, note, there exist a number of different settings).

B. The blessing of the people is by tradition reserved to the minister of Word and Sacrament. There is something here beyond a prayer, for it picks up on Christ's transmission of his authority to the apostles (cf. John 20). Blessing truly comes from God alone, who guides and 'in all things ... works for the good of those who love Him' (Romans 8:28). Thus the minister's work here is, strictly speaking, delegated; it is a mediated word and, for all that it is addressed in the 'you' form, obviously includes him or herself among those who are 'called out of darkness into God's marvellous light' (1 Peter 2:9). To be blessed is to be guided, shown the way, to be accompanied through all that awaits.

C. As the terms of this classic dismissal suggests, the continuing duties of God's people may be conceived of as cooperative or collaborative. Geographically, it may be given from the front or, also powerfully, by the minister physically coming into the midst of the people where space allows. Just as the liturgy has been a joint work in which God and people together have combined, so the so-called 'liturgy after the liturgy'. To be blessed is to become a blessing. We came together to worship God not simply for our own satisfaction. We are not sent out in that spirit either.

Strangely there is no mention in *Common Order* of one other traditional aspect at the end of a Communion service, namely the collection for the poor. The roots of this go back at least to Justin Martyr in the second century, and then of course to Jesus' teaching. In that offerings during the service tend to go into a central pot (see section 19 above), many congregations have retained the practice of a second, retiring offering which may be separately accounted for, perhaps in a Kirk Session Benevolent Fund, or the like. In some urban settings, there will be people looking for charity literally on the church steps. How we may be of service to the last and the least is a critical aspect of our Christianity, not least as we look forward to Christ coming again (cf. Matthew 25). There will have to be significant actions outside the church doors as well as when we gather together in Christ's name.

The spirit of love and mutual caring so much at the heart of the Sacrament should not be confined within the ecclesial gathering. In some places, there will be an immediate and welcome opportunity to adjourn for informal fellowship over refreshments. And between Sundays, the life of the kingdom of God is also to be anticipated – at all times and in all places.

'Blest are they, the poor in spirit ...' (*CH4*, no. 341)

QUESTION FOR DISCUSSION

How will the blessed community of faith 'shine for all to see'?

33 The removal of the bread and wine

The bread and wine are taken from the Church, the people standing.

A. Though in some situations the remaining bread and wine would be taken from the church during the last hymn, it is altogether better for them to be processed out rather after the Blessing, so that the whole community keeps together to the end. Some will traditionally at this point sing a Skailing hymn – a doxology, or 'Lord, thou lettest thy servant depart in peace', Simeon's prayer. It would be regular to maintain reverence before these gifts which were consecrated to a holy use and mystery.

B. Because it is rare for the bread and wine all to have been consumed before this point, thought should be given, as already noted, to what then happens to them. Ecumenical sensitivities come into play here, where there is great concern as to the too casual disposal of consecrated bread and wine, even while we may yet hold to Reformed tradition in suspicions about retaining anything for subsequent veneration ('any pretended religious use'). There are obvious options. One is that they should be consumed with thanksgiving by those who are charged with clearing up, so that there is no sense of being profligate with God's good gifts; indeed, the possibility should be there for anyone to help with that, in recognition that God's grace is overflowing. Another possibility is that they might be well used elsewhere. Some would feed bread to the birds, and pour the wine on the earth, in respect for all of God's creation. Some also, given that the Sacrament is to be shared with those who for reasons of health could not manage to be present at the main celebration, may take some of the leftover bread and wine. The minister and perhaps an elder or some other member(s) will go to visit such people in their homes and the event of the Lord's Supper will begin once again, although probably in a simple form. In that the whole action brings about the holiness of the Supper, whereby people come together for prayer and ascend through that to be met by Christ as the one raised to sit at the right hand of God, we would hold back from supposing that the elements of bread and wine can be carried around in consecrated form; nevertheless, to use the same bread and wine which was set apart for the 'holy use and mystery' in the main church assembly can reinforce the sense of longed-for connectedness by those who ask for this home communion to take place.[86]

C. The Sacrament of the Lord's Supper is about bread and wine in that these are 'figures', or in Calvin's terms 'signs and evidences' for the presence of Christ. What happens to them within the holy mystery is entirely by the grace of God. Whether we avouch the fourth-century bishop Ambrose or the radical Reformer Huldrych Zwingli, it is Christ's words which are 'performative', i.e. the ground and cause of what happens in the Supper.[87] Longing for the day when Christians will no longer separate around celebrations of the Lord's Supper, what we are asked to do is to unite and to hold together, through faith, the gospel of our Saviour Christ. Let the Supper be an epiphany, not a dreaded or burdensome routine – truly, then, the work of the Holy Spirit, although our knowledge of how much God loves us is still partial (cf. 1 Corinthians 13). There is at the end, therefore, more than enough

86 The 1940 *Book of Common Order* seemed to allow for consecratedness being portable; the more recent editions of *Common Order* have held back from that, though shorter forms of liturgy have been specifically provided. It remains the case that Communion in a home setting is not so appropriate for anyone able to join the larger worshipping assemblies. P. Tovey, *The Theory and Practice of Extended Communion* (Ashgate, 2009), gives an account of Roman Catholic, Methodist and Anglican perspectives in this area.

87 Jasper and Cuming (eds), *Prayers of the Eucharist*, pp. 112, 132.

good reason not to fuss over details: yet, we should not for an instant underplay the extraordinary nature of what we have been called to be part of.

Praise God, from whom all blessings flow;
praise Him, all creatures here below;
praise Him above, ye heavenly host,
praise Father, Son and Holy Ghost.

Thomas Ken (1637–1711)

Acknowledgements

Founded in 1948, the World Council of Churches is now a fellowship of more than 340 Christian churches confessing together 'the Lord Jesus Christ according to the scriptures' and seeking 'to fulfill together their common calling to the glory of the one God, Father, Son and Holy Spirit'. Tracing its origins to international movements dedicated to world mission and evangelism, life and work, faith and order, Christian education and church unity, the World Council is made up primarily of Protestant and Orthodox churches. The Roman Catholic Church is not a member church, but participates with the World Council of Churches and its member communions in a variety of activities and dialogues.

Lightning Source UK Ltd.
Milton Keynes UK
UKHW010503250719
346752UK00002B/149/P

9 780861 533992